stitch*style*

Socks

First published in the UK in 2007 by
Collins & Brown
10 Southcombe Street
London
W14 0RA

An imprint of Anova Books Company Ltd

Commissioning Editor: Michelle Lo
Design Manager: Gemma Wilson
Photographer: Mario Guarino
Designer: Clare Barber
Editor: Marie Clayton
Assistant Editor: Katie Hudson
Illustrator: Kang Chen
Senior Production Controller: Morna McPherson

Reproduction by Spectrum Colour Ltd, UK
Printed and bound by SNP Leefung, China

Martingale®
& C O M P A N Y

Martingale & Company
20205 144th Ave. NE
Woodinville, WA 98072-8478 USA
www.martingale-pub.com

Printed in China
07 06 05 04 03 02   8 7 6 5 4 3 2 1

Library of Congress Cataloging-in-Publication
Data Is Available

ISBN: 978-1-56477-827-7

stitch style

Twenty
Fashion
Knit and
Crochet
Styles

Socks

Martingale®
& COMPANY

Introduction

From trendy teenage girls to thirtysomething professionals, everyone is hand stitching these days. **Stitch Style Socks** is a collection of contemporary and urban projects that'll keep you constantly inspired, motivated, and putting your best foot forward. Each project is accompanied by full-color photography and easy-to-follow instructions. From striped laced knee-highs to pom-pom-embellished anklets, there's a style here for every season and occasion. Best of all, projects are portable so you're free to knit anywhere you go. **Stitch Style Socks** is designed for fashion-loving handcrafters, and features an array of hip styles inspired by everything from catwalks to street fashion. All designs are created by young urban knitters and trendsetters with a penchant for craft.

Contents

DESIGNED BY TANIS GRAY

Mary Jane Socks

These traditional Mary Jane socks are worked in one piece, starting at the back heel, with a separate crocheted strap. The button is for decoration only and does not unfasten.

YARN

A: 1 ball of Rowan *Handknit Cotton* (100% cotton; 50 g; 85 m), color 315 Double Choc

B: 1 ball of Rowan *Handknit Cotton*, color 316 Slippery

C: 1 ball of Rowan *Handknit Cotton*, color 318 Seafarer

D: 1 ball of Rowan *Handknit Cotton*, color 205 Linen

E: 1 ball of Rowan *Handknit Cotton*, color 313 Slick

NEEDLES

US 6 (4.00 mm) knitting needles

Size G/6 (4.25 mm) crochet hook

EXTRAS

2 buttons, ½ in. (12 mm) in diameter   Stitch holder   Tapestry needle

Sewing needle and thread

GAUGE

18 sts and 28 rows = 4 in. (10 cm) in St st on US 6 (4.00 mm) needles

TO FIT	SKILL LEVEL
Women's shoe size 6–9	Intermediate

SOCKS (Make 2)

Starting under the heel and using *temporary* cast-on technique with waste yarn, CO 6 sts.

Row 1: Using A, knit,
Row 2: K1, M1, K4, M1, K1.
Row 3: P1, M1, P6, M1, P1.
Row 4: K1, M1, K8, M1, K1.
Row 5: P1, M1, P10, M1, P1.
Join E.
Row 6: Using E, K1, M1, K12, M1, K1.
Join B.
Row 7: Using B, P1, M1, P14, M1, P1.
Row 8: K1, M1, K16, M1, K1. (20 sts)
Row 9: Purl.
Row 10: Knit.
Join E.
Row 11: Using E, purl.
Join C.
Rows 12–15: Using C, work even in St st.
Row 16: Using E, knit.
Join D.
Rows 17–20: Using D, work even in St st.
Row 21: Using E, purl.
Rows 22–25: Using A, work even in St st.
Row 26: Using E, knit.
Rows 27–56: Cont in color patt, work even in St st.
Row 57: Using D, purl.
Row 58: Knit.

TOE SHAPING

Row 59: P1, P2tog, P14, P2tog, P1.
Row 60: K1, K2tog, K12, K2tog, K1.

Row 61: Using E, P1, P2tog, P10, P2tog, P1.

Row 62: Using A, K1, K2tog, K8, K2tog, K1.

Row 63: P1, P2tog, P6, P2tog, P1.

Row 64: K1, K2tog, K4, K2tog, K1. (6 sts)

Row 65: Purl.

Rows 66–68: Using A, work even in St st.

Row 69: P1, M1, P4, M1, P1.

Row 70: K1, M1, K6, M1, K1.

Row 71: P1, M1, P8, M1, P1.

Row 72: K1, M1, K10, M1, K1.

Row 73: Using E, P1, M1, P12, M1, P1.

Row 74: Using D, K1, M1, K14, M1, K1. (18 sts)

Rows 75–77: Work even in St st.

Row 78: Using E, knit.

Row 79: Using C, purl.

Rows 80–82: Work even in St st.

Row 83: Using E, purl.

Row 84: Using B, knit.

Rows 85–87: Work even in St st.

Row 88: Using E, K5, place first 4 sts on holder, BO 10 sts, K3.

Row 89: Using A, P4.

Rows 90–92: Work even in St st.

Row 93: Using E, P4.

Rows 94–97: Using D, work even in St st.

Row 98: Using E, K4.

Rows 99–102: Using C, work even in St st.

Row 103: Using E, P4.

Rows 104–107: Using B, work even in St st.

Row 108: Using E, K4.

Rows 109–112: Using A, work even in St st.

Row 113: Using E, P4.

Rows 114–117: Using D, work even in St st.

ANKLE SHAPING

Row 118: Using E, K4, CO 10 sts, place these sts on holder.

Work on 4 sts from first holder, rep rows 89–117 on other side.

Join both sides. (18 sts)

Rows 119–122: Using C, work even in St st.

Row 123: Using E, P18.

Row 124: Using B, K18.

Row 125: P18.

HEEL SHAPING

Row 126: K18.

Row 127: P1, P2tog, P12, P2tog, P1.

Row 128: Using E, K1, K2tog, K10, K2tog, K1.

Row 129: Using A, P1, P2tog, P8, P2tog, P1.

Row 130: K1, K2tog, K6, K2tog, K1.

Row 131: P1, P2tog, P4, P2tog, P1.

Row 132: K1, K2tog, K2, K2tog, K1. (6 sts)

Row 133: P6.

Remove *temporary* cast on and, using 3-needle BO (at right), close heel.

FINISHING

Using sewing thread and needle, turn work inside out and sew up side seams. Weave in all loose yarn ends with tapestry needle. Using crochet hook and E, work sc around foot opening.

STRAP

Using crochet hook and E, sc a strap 6 in. (15 cm) lengthwise for 5 rows. Attach one side to inside of sock, securing with sewing thread and needle. Sew button onto opposite side of strap, then secure strap down with sewing thread and needle.

SPECIAL TECHNIQUE

3-needle BO: Hold two LH knitting needles tog with right sides of work facing each other. With a third needle, knit first st on front and back needles tog. Knit next st on front and back needles tog and bind off as normal by bringing loop of first st over second.

TIPS

- Iron nonslip "stickies" onto the bottom to prevent sliding.

- Sew strap on last; try on sock to ensure proper length and a snug fit.

- Socks can be made in any stripe, Fair Isle, or solid pattern.

DESIGNED BY ALISON DUPERNEX

Fleur-de-lis Slippers

These pretty fleur-de-lis slippers are knitted throughout in simple stockinette stitch. You just follow the charts to work the patterns.

YARN

A: 1 ball of Rowan *Felted Tweed* 50% merino/25% alpaca/25% viscose; 50 g; 175 m), color 133 Midnight

B: 1 ball of Rowan *Felted Tweed*, color 151 Bilberry

C: 1 ball of Rowan *Felted Tweed*, color 142 Sigh

D: 1 ball of Rowan *Felted Tweed*, color 155 Pickle

E: 1 ball of Rowan *Felted Tweed*, color 157 Camel

F: 1 ball of Rowan *Scottish Tweed* 4 ply (100% wool; 50 g; 110 m), color F016 Thistle

G: 1 ball of Rowan *Felted Tweed*, color G013 Claret

NEEDLES

US 6 (4.00 mm) knitting needles

GAUGE

24 sts and 32 rows = 4 in. (10 cm) in St st on US 6 (4.00 mm) needles

---

TO FIT	**SKILL LEVEL**
Women's shoe size 6–9	Intermediate

FLEUR-DE-LIS BODY

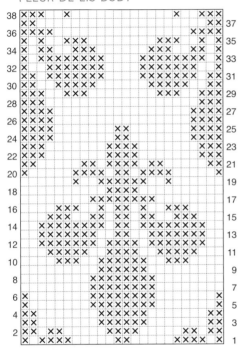

SOLE AND HEEL

CUFF

See stripe sequence (right) for color placement.

STRIPE SEQUENCE
FOR FLEUR-DE-LIS

For the slipper upper section, using fleur-de-lis chart, beg with a knit row and work in the following color sequence:

Rows 1–2: B.
Rows 3–8: B for background; D for x.
Rows 9–12: A for background; D for x.
Rows 13–16: C for background; D for x.
Rows 17–18: C for background; E for x.
Rows 19–22: C for background; D for x.
Rows 23–26: F for background; D for x.
Rows 27–30: B for background; D for x.
Rows 31–34: A for background; D for x.
Rows 35–36: A for background; E for x.
Rows 37–38: F for background; E for x.
Rows 39–40: F for background; D for x.
Rows 41–44: B for background; D for x.
Rows 45–50: A for background; D for x.

SLIPPER (Make 2)

UPPER SECTION

Using B and US 6 (4.00 mm) needles, CO 38 sts.

Rows 1–33: Work in St st. Follow stripe sequence and work chart for fleur-de-lis patt.

TOE SHAPING

Rows 34–49: Keeping patt correct, dec 1 st at beg of each row until 22 sts rem.

SOLE SHAPING

Follow chart for sole and heel, keeping patt correct while shaping.

Rows 50–65: With A for background and B for X, inc 1 st at beg of each row until there are 38 sts on needle.

Rows 66–122: Work even without shaping.

HEEL SHAPING

Rows 123–136: Cont in patt as set, dec 1 st at each end of every row until 10 sts rem.

Rows 137–151: With A for background and D for X, inc 1 st at each end of every row until 40 sts are on needle.

Rows 152–153: Work in St st with A. BO.

SLIPPER CUFF

Using E and US 6 (4.00 mm) needles, CO 72 sts and knit 1 row.

Row 2: Change to A, purl.

Rows 3–7: Follow cuff chart, with A for background and G for X.

Row 8: With A, purl.

Rows 9–10: Work in St st with E.

Rows 11–19: Work in St st with A. BO.

FINISHING

Fold the upper back over the sole and join the sloped side of the toe with the corresponding slopes of the sole. Rep with the heel. Fold the cuff in half and whipstitch in place around the top of the slipper, joining the seam at the side.

> ### TIP
> To make a larger size, simply add a few extra stitches to the width and a few extra rows to the length.

DESIGNED BY LYNN SERPE

Striper Socks

These snazzy socks use so little of each color that many pairs can be made with the quantities given. Try changing the colors around for a completely different pair of socks using the same pattern.

YARN

Rowan *Wool Cotton* (50% merino wool/50% cotton; 50 g; 113 m) in the following amounts and colors:

A: 1 ball of color 943 Flower
B: 1 ball of color 946 Elf
C: 1 ball of color 908 Inky
D: 1 ball of color 900 Antique
E: 1 ball of color 948 Poster Blue
F: 1 ball of color 962 Pumpkin
G: 1 ball of color 910 Gypsy
H: 1 ball of color 901 Citron
I: 1 ball of color 911 Rich
J: 1 ball of color 958 Aloof

NEEDLES

Set of 4 US 4 (3.50 mm) double-pointed needles

EXTRAS

Stitch markers

GAUGE

24 sts and 32 rows = 4 in. (10 cm) in St st on US 4 (3.50 mm) needles

TO FIT

Women's shoe size 6–9

SKILL LEVEL

Intermediate

SOCKS

Using A, CO 48 sts. Divide sts evenly across 3 dpns, join for working in the rnd.

Rnds 1–6: Work in K1, P1 ribbing.

Rnd 7: Knit.

Cut A, join B.

Rnds 8–10: Knit.

Cut B. Using Fair Isle technique, work as follows:

Rnds 11–13: (K2 with C; K2 with D); rep to end.

Rnds 14–16: (K2 with D; K2 with C); rep to end. Cut C and D.

Rnds 17–19: Knit with B. Cut B.

Rnds 20–21: Knit with E. Cut E.

Rnds 22–23: Knit with F. Cut F.

Rnds 24–25: Knit with G. Cut G.

Rnds 26–27: Knit with H. Cut H.

Rnds 28–29: Knit with I. Cut I.

Rnds 30–31: Knit with J. Cut J.

Rnd 32: Knit with A.

Rnd 33: K12, pm, K24, pm, K12.

Cut A.

HEEL FLAP

Rearrange sts for knitting heel flap by placing 24 sts between markers on one needle (to be worked later). Place 12 sts before first marker and 12 sts after second marker on one needle to be knit back and forth for heel flap.

Row 1: (K1, sl 1) with A to end of row.

Row 2: Purl.

Rep last 2 rows until heel flap measures 2½ in. (6.25 cm).

HEEL TURN

Next row: K12, pm, K12.

Next row: Purl to marker, sm, P2, P2tog, P1.

Next row: Knit to marker, sm, K2, K2tog, K1.

Remove marker in next row.

Next row: P7, P2tog, P1.

Next row: K8, K2tog, K1.

Next row: P9, P2tog, P1.

Next row: K10, K2tog, K1.

Next row: P11, P2tog, P1.

Next row: K12, K2tog, K1.

Next row: P13, P2tog.

Next row: K13, K2tog. (14 sts).

Cut A.

FOOT

Rnd 1: With D, pick up and K12 along right side of heel flap, K7 of heel sts (N1), K7 of rem heel sts, pick up and K12 along left side of heel flap (N2), K24 sts on holding needle (N3).

Rnd 2: With C, ssk, knit to last 2 sts on N2, K2tog, knit to end of rnd.

Rnd 3: Knit with D.

Rep last 2 rnds until 48 sts rem.

Next rnd: Knit with C.

Next rnd: Knit with D.

Rep last 2 rnds until foot measures 6½ in. (16.25 cm) from back of heel or 2 in. (5 cm) shorter than desired length of foot. Cut C and D.

TOE

Rnd 1: Knit with A.

Rnd 2: Knit to last 3 sts of N3, ssk, K1.

Rnd 3: K1, K2tog, knit to last 3 sts of N2, ssk, K2, K2tog, knit to end of rnd.

Rep last 2 rnds until 32 sts rem.

Next rnd: Knit to last 3 sts of N3, ssk, K1.

Next rnd: K1, K2tog, knit to last 3 sts of N2, ssk, K2, K2tog, knit to last 3 sts of N3, ssk, K1.

Rep last rnd until 19 sts rem.

Next rnd: K1, K2tog, knit to last 3 sts of N2, ssk, K2, K2tog, knit to end of rnd. (16 sts)

Graft sts tog using kitchener st.

TIPS

- Throughout the pattern, take care in switching colors so as not to leave a hole in the fabric.

- For the stripe portion of the foot, it is not necessary to cut the yarn after every round. You can twist the old yarn with the new before the first stitch of each round.

DESIGNED BY STEPHANIE MRSE

Skull Socks

Bring out your swashbuckling pirate nature with these skull-motif socks, knitted in the softest yarn to please even the most hard-hearted pirate.

YARN

MC: 3 balls of Debbie Bliss *Merino DK* (100% merino wool; 50 g; 110 m), color 300 Black

A: 1 ball of Debbie Bliss *Merino DK,* color 100 White

NEEDLES	**EXTRAS**
Set of 5 US 2 (3.00 mm) double-pointed needles	Stitch markers
Set of 5 US 3 (3.25 mm) double-pointed needles	

GAUGE

26 sts and 34 rows = 4 in. (10 cm) in St st on US 3 (3.25 mm) needles

---

TO FIT	**SKILL LEVEL**
Women's shoe size 6–9	Advanced

SOCKS (Make 2)
LEG
Using MC and US 2 (3.00 mm) needles, loosely CO 64 sts. Divide evenly onto 4 needles, being careful not to twist sts. Work in K2, P2 ribbing for 1½ in. (4 cm). Change to US 3 (3.25 mm) needles and knit 1 row, pm after first 4 sts and before last 4 sts.

Working first and last 4 sts in MC, knit chart rnds 1–16 once.

Knit chart rnds 1–12 once.

Start dec:

Start dec, cont in patt as set:

Rnd 13a (chart): K1, K2tog, knit to last 3 sts, ssk, K1. (62 sts)

Rnd 14a (chart): Knit.

Rnd 15a (chart): Rep rnd 13a. (60 sts)

Rnd 16a (chart): Knit.

Knit rnds 1–12 of chart once.

Rnd 13b (chart): K2tog, knit to last 2 sts, ssk. (58 sts)

Rnd 14b (chart): Knit.

Rnd 15b (chart): Rep rnd 13b. (56 sts)

Rnd 16b (chart): Knit.

Knit chart rnds 1–16 once.

Rnd 17: K1, K2tog, knit to last 3 sts, ssk, K1. (54 sts)

Rnd 18: Knit.

Rnd 19: K1, K2tog, knit to last 3 sts, ssk, K1. (52 sts)

Rnd 20: Knit.

Rnd 21: K2tog, knit to last 2 sts, ssk. (50 sts)

Rnd 22: Knit.

Rnd 23: Rep rnd 21. (48 sts)

Cont to knit even until work measures 12 in. (30.5 cm) from CO or desired length.

HEEL FLAP
(Work over center back 24 sts back and forth)

Row 1: (Sl 1 kw, K1) 12 times.

Row 2: Sl 1 pw, P23.

Rep rows 1–2 until heel flap measures 2½ in. (6.5 cm), ending with row 2.

HEEL TURN
Next row: Sl 1, K13, ssk, K1, turn.

Next row: Sl 1, P5, P2tog, P1, turn.

Next row: Sl 1, K6, ssk, K1, turn.

Next row: Sl 1, P7, P2tog, P1, turn.

Cont in this manner until all sts are worked. (14 sts)

Next row: K14.

GUSSETS
Pick up 14 sts along side of heel flap, knit across 24 sts of instep, pick up 14 sts along other side of heel flap. Divide heel sts between N1 and N4.

Rnd 1: Knit.

Rnd 2

    N1: Knit to last 3 sts, K2tog, K1.

    N2: K12.

    N3: K12.

    N4: K1, ssk, knit rem sts.

Rep rnds 1–2 until a total of 48 sts rem.

☐ A

■ MC

The socks are knit in the round and the chart is worked from right to left, but for the sake of legibility, row numbers are shown at both right and left in the chart.

FOOT
Work even until foot measures about 2 in. (5 cm) shorter than desired length of sock.

TOE SHAPING
Rnd 1

    N1: Knit to last 3 sts, K2tog, K1.

    N2: K1, ssk, knit rem sts.

    N3: Knit to last 3 sts, K2tog, K1.

    N4: K1, ssk, knit rem sts.

Rnd 2: Knit.

Rep rnds 1–2 until a total of 20 sts rem. Cut yarn, leaving a 12 in. (30.5 cm) tail for weaving.

FINISHING
Weave toe tog with kitchener st. Weave in all ends.

DESIGNED BY STEPHANIE MRSE

I ♥ Socks

These are cute little heart socks with real cheerleader style! For longer socks, knit the chart section two or more times.

YARN

MC: 2 balls of Debbie Bliss *Merino DK* (100% merino wool; 50 g; 110 m), color 100 White

A: 1 ball of Debbie Bliss *Merino DK,* color 608 Purple

B: 1 ball of Debbie Bliss *Merino DK,* color 700 Red

NEEDLES

Set of 5 US 3 (3.25 mm) double-pointed needles

GAUGE

---

26 sts and 34 rows = 4 in. St st on US 3 (3.25 mm) needles

TO FIT	**SKILL LEVEL**
Women's shoe size 6–9	Advanced

SOCKS (Make 2)

CUFF
With MC, loosely CO 48 sts.
Divide sts evenly between 4 needles, being careful not to twist sts.
Knit in K2, P2 ribbing for 1 ½ in. (4 cm).
Next rnd: Knit.
Knit heart and stripes chart once.
Knit 5 rnds in A.

HEEL FLAP
Work over 24 sts with A as follows:
Row 1: (Sl 1 kw, K1) 12 times.
Row 2: Sl 1 pw, P23.
Rep rows 1 and 2 until heel flap measures 2½ in. (6.5 cm), ending with row 2.

HEEL TURN
Next row: Sl 1, K13, ssk, K1, turn.
Next row: Sl 1, P5, P2tog, P1, turn.
Next row: Sl 1, K6, ssk, K1, turn.
Next row: Sl 1, P7, P2tog, P1, turn.
Cont in this manner, inc the sts worked by 1 each time until all side sts are used. (14 sts)
Next row: K7, switch to A, K7.

GUSSET
Pick up 14 sts along side of heel flap, knit across 24 sts of instep, pick up 14 sts along other side of heel flap. Divide heel sts between N1 and N4.
Rnd 1: Knit.

Rnd 2

N1: Knit to last 3 sts, K2tog, K1.
N2 and N3: K12.
N4: K1, ssk, knit rem sts.
Rep rnds 1 and 2 until 48 sts rem.

FOOT

Work even until foot measures about 2 in. (5 cm) shorter than desired length of sock.

TOE SHAPING

Work toe with B.
Rnd 1

N1: Knit to last 3 sts, K2tog, K1.
N2: K1, ssk, knit rem sts.
N3: Knit to last 3 sts, K2tog, K1.
N4: K1, ssk, knit rem sts.
Rnd 2: Knit.
Rep rnds 1 and 2 until 20 sts rem.
Cut yarn, leaving a 12 in. (30.5 cm) tail for weaving.

FINISHING

Weave toe tog with kitchener st. Weave in all ends.

□ MC
▨ A
▨ B

The socks are knit in the round and the chart is worked from right to left, but for the sake of legibility, row numbers are shown at both right and left in the chart.

TIP

You might want to go up one needle size when working the chart, since Fair Isle tends to pull in the fabric and is less stretchy than regular stockinette stitch.

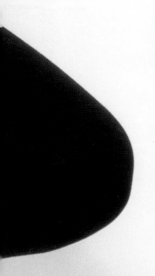

DESIGNED BY JUDY FURLONG

Houndstooth Socks

These smart plaid socks, knitted in tweedy wool, have a neat ribbing edge. For a different look, work a longer ribbing and turn it over to form a cuff.

YARN

MC: 3 balls of Rowan *Scottish Tweed 4 ply* (100% wool; 25 g; 110 m), color 23 Midnight

A: 2 balls of Rowan *Scottish Tweed 4 ply*, color 24 Porridge

NEEDLES

Set of 4 US 3 (3.25 mm) double-pointed needles
Set of 4 US 2 (2.75 mm) double-pointed needles

EXTRAS

Stitch marker
Yarn needle

GAUGE

28 sts and 32 rows = 4 in. (10 cm) in shepherd's plaid patt on US 3 (3.25 mm) needles

TO FIT

Women's shoe size 6–9

SKILL LEVEL

Intermediate

SPECIAL ABBREVIATIONS

ik2tog: Insert tip of RH needle into st immediately below next st, pick it up and put it on LH needle. Knit it tog with next st.

ip2tog: Insert tip of RH needle into st immediately below next st, pick it up and put it on LH needle. Purl into back of it tog with next st.

sl 1p: Slip 1 st pw.

SOCKS (Make 2)

Using US 2 (2.75 mm) needles and MC, CO 64 sts.

Place 21 sts on each of first 2 needles and 22 sts on third needle.

Work 1¼ in. (3 cm) in K1, P1 ribbing, dec 1 st at end of last rnd. (63 sts)

Change to US 3 (3.25 mm) needles and beg working in St st.

Work shepherd's plaid patt:

Join A and, starting with rnd 1, follow the chart until 6 reps of the patt (48 rows) have been completed and sock measures 7 in. (17.5 cm) from CO edge.

Divide for heel and instep:

With MC only, K32. Slip these 32 sts onto the same needle and cont in MC on these sts only for the heel.

HEEL

Row 1 (WS facing): Sl 1p, P31 (to end of needle), turn.

Row 2: Sl 1, K30 (1 st rem), turn.

Row 3: Sl 1p, P29 (1 st rem), turn.

Row 4: Sl 1, K28 (2 sts rem), turn.

Row 5: Sl 1p, P27 (2 sts rem), turn.

Row 6: Sl 1, K26 (3 sts rem), turn.

Row 7: Sl 1p, P25 (3 sts rem), turn.

Row 8: Sl 1, K24 (4 sts rem), turn.

Row 9: Sl 1p, P23 (4 sts rem), turn.

Row 10: Sl 1, K22 (5 sts rem), turn.

Row 11: Sl 1p, P21 (5 sts rem), turn.

Row 12: Sl 1, K20 (6 sts rem), turn.

Row 13: Sl 1p, P19 (6 sts rem), turn.

Row 14: Sl 1, K18 (7 sts rem), turn.

Row 15: Sl 1p, P17 (7 sts rem), turn.

Row 16: Sl 1, K16 (8 sts rem), turn.

Row 17: Sl 1p, P15 (8 sts rem), turn.

Row 18: Sl 1, K14 (9 sts rem), turn.

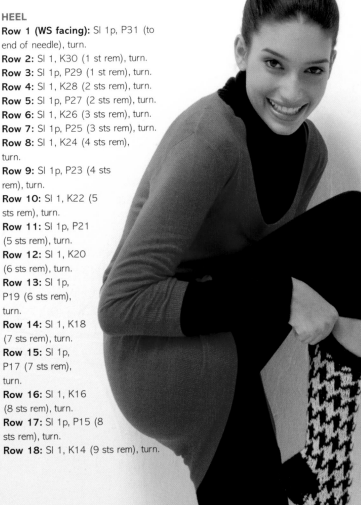

Row 19: Sl 1p, P13 (9 sts rem), turn.
Row 20: Sl 1, K12 (10 sts rem), turn.
Row 21: Sl 1p, P11 (10 sts rem), turn.
Row 22: K12, ik2tog (9 sts rem on left-hand needle), turn.
Row 23: P13, ip2tog (9 sts rem on left-hand needle), turn.
Row 24: K14, ik2tog, turn (8 sts rem).
Row 25: P15, ip2tog, turn (8 sts rem).
Row 26: K16, ik2tog, turn (7 sts rem).
Row 27: P17, ip2tog, turn (7 sts rem).
Row 28: K18, ik2tog, turn (6 sts rem).
Row 29: P19, ip2tog, turn (6 sts rem).
Row 30: K20, ik2tog, turn (5 sts rem).
Row 31: P21, ip2tog, turn (5 sts rem).
Row 32: K22, ik2tog, turn (4 sts rem).
Row 33: P23, ip2tog, turn (4 sts rem).
Row 34: K24, ik2tog, turn (3 sts rem).
Row 35: P25, ip2tog, turn (3 sts rem).
Row 36: K26, ik2tog, turn (2 sts rem).
Row 37: P27, ip2tog, turn (2 sts rem).
Row 38: K28, ik2tog, turn (1 st rem).
Row 39: P29, ip2tog, turn (1 st rem).
Row 40: K30, ik2tog (no sts rem), turn.
Row 41: P31, ip2tog (no sts rem), turn.
Rearrange these sts so first 21 sts rem on first needle and rem 11 sts are slipped onto second needle. There should now be 21 sts on each needle. Working with both colors and starting with rnd 1, work in shepherd's plaid patt, following chart, until 6 rep of patt (48 rows) have been completed.

TOE SHAPING

Break off A and cont in MC only.
Rnd 1: K1, skpo, K12, K2tog, K12, K2tog, K2, skpo, K25, K2tog, K1. (58 sts)
Rnd 2: K29, pm, K29.
Rnd 3: K1, skpo, knit to 3 sts before marker, K2tog, K1, sm, K1, skpo, knit to 3 sts before end of rnd, K2tog, K1. (54 sts)
Rnd 4: Knit.
Rnds 5–12: Rep last 2 rnds 4 more times. (38 sts)
Rnds 13–16: Rep rnd 3 another 4 times. (22 sts)
Sl the first 11 sts onto 1 needle and the remaining 11 sts onto a 2nd needle. Graft tog.

FINISHING

Weave in loose ends. Pin out according to measurement. Lightly steam or press with a pressing cloth, avoiding ribbing.

The socks are knit in the round and the chart is worked from right to left, but for the sake of legibility, row numbers are shown at both right and left in the chart.

■ MC
□ A

DESIGNED BY SIMONA MERCHANT-DEST

Textured Socks with Flowers

A bouquet of leaves, flowers at the ankle, and a beaded edge to the cuff make pretty accents to these textured socks.

YARN

MC: 3 balls of Rowan Wool Cotton (50% wool/50% cotton; 50 g; 113 m), color 962 Pumpkin

A: 1 ball of Rowan Wool Cotton, color 911 Rich

B: 1 ball of Rowan Wool Cotton, color 907 Deepest Olive

NEEDLES

Set of 5 US 2 (2.75 mm) double-pointed needles

Size E/4 (3.50 mm) crochet hook

EXTRAS

24 drop beads	Stitch marker
24 green 6/0 E beads	Tapestry needle
30 orangish yellow 6/0 E beads	Sewing needle

GAUGE

22 sts and 32 rows = 4 in. (10 cm) in St st or cellular st on US 2 (2.75 mm) needles

TO FIT

Women's shoe size 6–9

SKILL LEVEL

Intermediate

SOCKS (Make 2)

CUFF

Using US 2 (2.75 mm) needles and MC, CO 48 sts and divide them equally over 4 needles (12 sts on each). Join into circle without twisting sts, pm to indicate beg of rnd.

Rnd 1: *K2, P2; rep from * to end.

Rnds 2–33: Cont in ribbing as set or until cuff measures 4½ in. (11 cm) from beg.

LEG

Rnd 1: *YO, K1, YO, sl 1, K2tog, psso; rep from * to end.

Rnd 2: Knit.

Rnd 3: *Sl 1, K2tog, psso, YO, K1, YO; rep from * to end.

Rnd 4: Knit.

Rep rnds 1–4 until piece measures 10 in. (25 cm) from beg.

Knit sts on first dpn; leave sts on second and third dpns on hold. From now on, you will work sts from fourth and first dpns only.

HEEL FLAP

Put sts from first and fourth dpns on 1 dpn. Now work in rows on 24 sts.

Row 1 (WS): Purl.

Row 2: Sl 1 pw wyib, knit to end.

Row 3: Sl 1 pw wyif, purl to end.

Rep rows 2 and 3 another 8 times or until the heel flap measures 2 in. (5 cm). (18 rows)

HEEL TURN

Row 1 (RS): K14, ssk, K1, turn.
Row 2: Sl 1, P5, P2tog, P1, turn.
Row 3: Sl 1, K6, ssk, K1, turn.
Row 4: Sl 1, P7, P2tog, P1, turn.
Row 5: Sl 1, K8, ssk, K1, turn.
Row 6: Sl 1, P9, P2tog, P1, turn.
Row 7: Sl 1, K10, ssk, K1, turn.
Row 8: Sl 1, P11, P2tog, P1, turn.
Row 9: Sl 1, K12, ssk, turn.
Row 10: P13, P2tog; turn. (14 sts)

GUSSET

Set-up rnd (RS): K14; then with same needle, pick up 10 sts along side of heel flap and 1 additional st beyond flap to close gap. (25 sts)

Work 24 sts over 2nd and 3rd dpns with cellular patt as follows:
YO, K2tog, YO, sl 1, K2tog, psso; *YO, K1, YO, sl 1, K2tog, psso; rep from * to last 3 sts on 3rd dpn; YO, K1, YO, K2tog.
With fourth dpn, pick up 1 st between third dpn and heel flap to close gap, then pick up 10 sts along side of heel flap and K7 from first dpn. Now you have 4 dpns with 60 sts divided as follows: 18, 12, 12, 18 sts. Beg of rnd is the heel center.
Rnd 1: Knit.
Rnd 2
    First dpn: Knit.
    Second and third dpns: Work cellular patt as follows: *YO, sl 1, K2tog, psso, YO, K1; rep from * to heel.
    Fourth dpn: Knit.

Rnd 3

First dpn: Knit to last 3 sts, K2tog, K1.

Second and third dpns: Knit.

Fourth dpn: K1, ssk, knit to end. (dec total of 2 sts)

Rnd 4

First dpn: Knit.

Second and third dpns: Work cellular patt as follows: YO, K2tog, YO, sl 1, K2tog, psso; *YO, K1, YO, sl 1, K2tog, psso; rep from * to last 3 sts on third dpn, YO, K1, YO, K2tog.

Fourth dpn: Knit.

Rnd 5: Rep rnd 3.

Rep rnds 2–5 until you have a total of 48 sts left, then work as follows:

Next rnd: Knit.

Next rnd: Work as rnd 2 above.

Next rnd: Knit.

Next rnd: Work as rnd 4 above.

Cont until foot measures 7 in. (17.5 cm) or length of your foot minus 2 in. (5 cm), then start shaping toe.

TOE SHAPING

Rnds 1–2: Knit.

Rnd 3

First dpn: Knit to last 3 sts, K2tog, K1.

Second dpn: K1, ssk, knit to end.

Third dpn: As for first dpn.

Fourth dpn: As for second dpn. (dec total of 4 sts)

Rnd 4: Knit.

Rnds 5–12: Rep rnds 3 and 4. (28 sts)

Rnds 13–17: Rep rnd 3 only. (8 sts)

Break off yarn and thread it through tapestry needle. Thread yarn through live sts and pull tight to close. Weave in end.

FINISHING

LARGE FLOWERS (Make 2)

Using US 2 (2.75 mm) needles and A, CO 49 sts.

Rows 1–2: Knit.

Row 3: K1, *BO 7 sts, leave last bound-off st on RH needle; rep from * 5 more times. (7 sts)

Row 4: K7.

Break off yarn, thread through live sts to close rnd, then sew sides to form flower.

SMALL FLOWERS (Make 2)

Using US 2 (2.75 mm) needles and A, CO 21 sts.

Row 1: K1, *BO 3 sts, leave last bound-off st on RH needle; rep from * 4 more times. (6 sts)

Break off yarn, thread through live sts to close rnd, then sew sides to form flower.

LEAVES (Make 6)

Using US 2 (2.75 mm) needles and B, CO 3 sts.

Row 1 (WS): Purl.

Row 2: K1, YO, K1, YO, K1. (5 sts)

Row 3: Purl.

Row 4: K2, YO, K1, YO, K2. (7 sts)

Row 5: Purl.

Row 6: Ssk, K3, K2tog. (5 sts)

Row 7: Purl.

Row 8: Ssk, K1, K2tog. (3 sts)

Row 9: Purl.

Row 10: K3tog.

Fasten off.

Arrange flowers and leaves, referring to photo for positioning, and sew onto socks. Split a length of yarn in half, thread through sewing needle, and sew beads onto large flowers as shown.

FRINGE

Using E/4 (3.50 mm) hook and MC, sc around edge of cuff. Fasten off. Weave in ends. Cut yarn MC into 12 pieces, 6 in. (15 cm) long; fold each piece in half and tie onto edge of cuff, spacing equally, with 2 ends coming out of each tie. *Tie one end of a fringe with end of fringe next to it into a knot; rep from * until all ends are tied into knots. Trim ends to same lengths close to knot.

BEADS

Split a length of yarn in half, thread through sewing needle and sew beads onto cuff as follows: go through cuff edge, thread on 1 green 6/0 E bead and 1 drop bead; with needle go back through the same green 6/0 E bead, then go through edge, creating a triangle (see photo); rep 11 more times. Weave in ends.

DESIGNED BY SUE BRADLEY

Beaded Leg Warmers

These snazzy striped leg warmers include beads for a touch of glitz. For an even more feminine look, decorate them by threading ribbons through the dropped rows.

YARN

A: 2 balls of Debbie Bliss Donegal *Aran Tweed* (100% wool; 50 g; 92 m), color 04 Light Beige

B: 1 ball of Rowan *Kid Classic* (70% lambs wool; 26% kid mohair, 4% nylon; 50 g; 140 m), color 828 Feather

C: 1 ball of Debbie Bliss *Donegal Aran Tweed*, color 02 Dark Grey

NEEDLES

US 8 (5.00 mm) knitting needles
US 7 (4.50 mm) knitting needles

EXTRAS

200 beads with large enough holes to thread on yarn

GAUGE

18 sts and 24 rows = 4 in. (10 cm) in St st on US 8 (5.00 mm) needles

TO FIT

Women's shoe size 6–9

SKILL LEVEL

Intermediate

SPECIAL ABBREVIATION

YRN2: Wrap yarn around needle twice
on each st.

LEG WARMERS (Make 2)

Using US 7 (4.50 mm) needles and B,
CO 48 sts and work in K4, P4 ribbing
for 14 rows.

Change to US 8 (5.00 mm) needles.

Row 1 (RS): Knit with C.

Row 2: Knit with C.

Row 3: Knit with B, YRN2.

Row 4: Knit with B, dropping YRN2.
Thread 48 beads onto yarn A.

Row 5: Knit with A.
Row 6: Knit with A and add bead on alternate sts. (24 beads used)
Rows 7–8: Knit with C.
Row 9: Knit with B, YRN2.
Row 10: Knit with B, dropping YRN2.
Row 11: Knit with A.
Row 12: Knit with A, add bead on alternate sts. (rem 24 beads used)
Row 13: Knit with C.
Row 14: Knit with C, YRN2.
Row 15: Knit with C, dropping YRN2. Break yarn C and thread on 24 beads.
Row 16: Knit with C, add bead on alternate sts.
Rows 17–22: Beg with a knit row, work in St st with A.
Row 23: Knit with B, YRN2.
Row 24: Purl with B, dropping YRN2.
Rows 25–32: Beg with a knit row, work in St st with A.
Rows 33–42: Rep rows 23–32.
Rows 43–44: Work in St st with A.
Row 45: Knit with C, YRN2.
Row 46: Purl with C, dropping YRN2.
Row 47: Knit with C.
Row 48: Purl with C.
Rows 49–58: Work in St st with A.
Row 59: Knit with B, YRN2.
Row 60: Knit with B, dropping YRN2.
Rows 61–64: Work in St st with B. Break yarn C and thread on 24 beads.
Rows 65–67: Knit with C.
Row 68: Knit with C, add bead on alternate sts.
Row 69: Knit with B, YRN2.
Row 70: Knit with B, dropping YRN2.
Rows 71–72: Knit with C.
Rows 73–74: Work in St st with C.
Row 75: Knit with A, YRN2.
Row 76: Purl with A, dropping YRN2.
Rows 77–82: Work St st with A.
Row 83: Knit with A, YRN2.
Row 84: Knit with A, dropping YRN2.
Rows 85–90: Work in St st with B.
Row 91: Knit with C, YRN2.
Row 92: Knit with C, dropping YRN2.
Rows 93–94: Work in St st with B.
Change to US 7 (4.50 mm) needles and yarn B and work in K4, P4 ribbing for 14 rows.
BO in ribbing.

FINISHING
Weave in all ends and sew the seams.

Vandyke Lace Socks

This lacy sock is worked from the toe up, with a band of pattern running up the leg and a pretty scalloped edge at the top.

YARN

3 balls of Rowan *Wool Cotton* (50% merino wool/50% cotton; 50 g; 113 m), color 943 Flower

NEEDLES

Set of 5 US 2 (2.75 mm) double-pointed needles

EXTRAS

Size B/1 (2.00 mm) crochet hook
Size D/3 (3.25 mm) crochet hook
Stitch markers
Tapestry needle

GAUGE

24 sts and 36 rows = 4 in. (10 cm) in St st on US 2 (2.75 mm) needles
24 sts and 30 rows = 4 in. (10 cm) in staggered eyelet st on US 2 (2.75 mm) needles
22 sts and 30 rows = 4 in. (10 cm) in Vandyke lace st on US 2 (2.75 mm) needles

TO FIT

Women's shoe size 6–9

SKILL LEVEL

Advanced

SOCKS
(Make 2 alike to beg of leg)
TOE

Using US 2 (2.75 mm) needles, CO 8 sts onto N1. Turn upside down, and with another dpn CO 7 sts on the CO-edge side, pulling sts through the spaces between the CO sts on N1. (15 sts)

Rnd 1: N1: K4; N2: K4; N3: K1, M1, K2; N4: K4, pm to indicate beg of rnd. (16 sts; 4 sts on each needle)

Rnd 2: *N1: K1, M1, knit to end; N2: knit to last st, M1, K1; rep from * once more for N3 and N4. (20 sts)

Rnds 3–4: Rep rnd 2. (28 sts)

Rnd 5: Knit.

Rnd 6: Rep rnd 2. (32 sts)

Rnds 7–18: Rep rnds 5–6 another 6 times. (56 sts)

Rnds 19–21: Knit; in the last rnd, dec 1 st. (55 sts)

FOOT

Start working the staggered eyelet patt over N1 and N2; cont St st over N3 and N4 as follows:

Rnd 1: (K2, K2tog, YO) 6 times, K3, knit to end of rnd.

Rnds 2–4: Knit.

Rnd 5: K4, (K2tog, YO, K2) 5 times, K3, knit to end of rnd.

Rnds 6–8: Knit.

Rep rnds 1–8 another 5 times or until piece measures 7 in. (17.5 cm) from toe or your foot length less 2 in. (5 cm). In the last rnd, work only to the last st on N4; bring the yarn in front as if to purl and sl the last st. Now leave sts on N1 and N2 on hold and work the heel shaping over N3 and N4 only.

HEEL
Row 1 (WS): Slip first unworked st from left dpn to right dpn (wrapping that first st around its base with the working yarn), purl to the last st, sl last st and bring yarn around to front, turn.
Row 2: Sl 1, knit to last worked st, bring yarn in front and sl last worked st as if to purl, bring yarn around to back, turn.
Row 3: Sl 1, purl to last worked st, sl 1, wrap yarn around, turn.
Rep rows 2–3 until there are 10 worked sts left and 9 slipped wrapped sts on each side.

HEEL TURN
Row 1 (RS): Knit all worked sts to first unworked wrapped st, pick up st with wrap and knit them tog. Sl next unworked st and wrap yarn around, turn.
Row 2: Sl 1 (double-wrapped) st and purl all worked sts, pick up wrap(s) and unworked st and purl them tog. Wrap the following unworked st and sl it, turn.

Row 3: Sl 1 (double-wrapped) st and knit all worked sts, pick up both wraps and unworked st and knit them tog. Sl next unworked st, wrap it around, turn.
Cont in this fashion, rep rows 2–3 until all unworked sts are worked and finishing with a WS row. (28 sts)

LEG

Start working over all dpns again.

Rnd 1: *K2, K2tog, YO; rep from * 5 more times, K3, M1, K to end. (56 sts)

Rnds 2–4: Knit.

Rnd 5: *K2tog, YO, K2; rep from * to end.

Rnds 6–8: Knit.

Rnd 9: *K2, K2tog, YO; rep from * to end.

Rnds 10–12: Knit.

Rnd 13: Rep rnd 5.

RIGHT SOCK

Rnds 14–16: Knit.

Rnd 17: (K2, K2tog, YO) 5 times, K7, YO, ssk, K5, K2tog, YO, (K2, K2tog, YO) 5 times.

Rnd 18: K19, pm, K17, pm, K20. *Note:* Work Vandyke lace between markers; work staggered eyelet st before and after markers.

Rnd 19: K19, sm, K6, K2tog, YO, K1, YO, ssk, K6, sm, K20.

Rnd 20 and each even rnd through 44: Knit.

Rnd 21: (K2tog, YO, K2) 4 times, K3, sm, K5, K2tog, YO, K3, YO, ssk, K5, sm, K4, (K2, K2tog, YO) 4 times.

Rnd 23: K19, sm, K2tog, YO, K1, YO, ssk, K3, YO, ssk, K2, K2tog, YO, K1, YO, ssk, sm, K20 to end.

Rnd 25: (K2, K2tog, YO) 4 times, K3, sm, (K2tog, YO, K1, YO, ssk, K1) twice, K2tog, YO, K1, YO, ssk, sm, (K2, K2tog, YO) 5 times.

Rnd 27: K19, sm, K2tog, YO, K1, YO, ssk, K2tog; YO, K3, YO, ssk, K2tog, YO, K1, YO, ssk, sm, K20.

Rnd 29: (K2tog, YO, K2) 4 times, K3, sm, K2tog, YO, K1, YO, ssk, K3, YO, ssk, K2, K2tog, YO, K1, YO, ssk, sm, K4, (K2tog, YO, K2) 4 times.

Rnd 31: K19, sm, (K2tog, YO, K1, YO, ssk, K1) twice, K2tog, YO, K1, YO, ssk, sm, K20.

Rnd 33: (K2, K2tog, YO) 4 times, K3, sm, K2tog, YO, K1, YO, ssk, K2tog, YO, K3, YO, ssk, K2tog, YO, K1, YO, ssk, (K2, K2tog, YO) 5 times.

Rnd 35: Rep rnd 23.

Rnd 37: (K2tog, YO, K2) 4 times, K3, sm, (K2tog, YO, K1, YO, ssk, K1) twice, K2tog, YO, K1, YO, ssk, sm, K4, (K2tog, YO, K2) 4 times.

Rnd 39: Rep rnd 27.

Rnd 41: (K2, K2tog, YO) 4 times, K3, sm, K2tog, YO, K1, YO, ssk, K3, YO, ssk, K2, K2tog, YO, K1, YO, ssk, sm, (K2, K2tog, YO) 5 times.

Rnd 43: Rep rnd 31.

Rnd 45: (K2tog, YO, K2) 4 times, K3, sm, K2tog, YO, K1, YO, ssk, K2tog, YO, K3, YO, ssk, K2tog, YO, K1, YO, ssk, sm, K4, (K2tog, YO, K2) 4 times.

Rnds 46–51: Knit.

Rnd 52: *K2, P2; rep from * to end.

Rnd 53: (K2, YO, P2tog, K2, P2, K2, P2tog, YO) twice, K2, YO, P2tog, K2, P2tog, YO, (K2, YO, P2tog, K2, P2, K2, P2tog, YO) twice.

Rnds 54–63: Cont in established ribbing patt *K2, P2; rep from * to end.

Rnds 64–65: Knit.

BO all sts. *Do not* cut yarn. Pick up rem st with size D/3 (3.25 mm) crochet hook and work sl st to finish BO rnd.

SCALLOPED EDGE

Rnd 1: *Ch 3, sk next 2 sc, 1 sc into next 2 sts; rep from * 13 more times to end.

Rnd 2: Work 5 sc into first ch-3 space, *5 sc into following ch-3 space; rep from * 12 more times.

LEFT SOCK

Rnds 1–13: As for leg.

Rnd 14 (set-up rnd): K8, pm, K40, pm; this marker marks *new* beg of rnd.

Rnd 15: Beg of rnd: knit rem 8 sts from N4 with new needle, knit to end. (*new* beg marker)

Rnd 16: Knit to last 2 sts, K2tog.

Rnd 17: Sm, YO, K7, YO, ssk, K5, K2tog, YO, sm, *K2, K2tog, YO; rep from * to last 3 sts, K3.

Rnd 18 and each even rnd through 44: Knit.

Rnd 19: Sm, K6, K2tog, YO, K1, YO, ssk, K6, sm, knit to end.

Rnd 21: Sm, K5, K2tog, YO, K3, YO, ssk, K5, sm, K4, *K2tog, YO, K2; rep from * to last 3 sts, K3.

Rnd 23: Sm, K2tog, YO, K1, YO, ssk, K3, YO, ssk, K2, K2tog, YO, K1, YO, ssk, sm, knit to end.

Rnd 25: Sm, (K2tog, YO, K1, YO, ssk, K1) twice, K2tog, YO, K1, YO, ssk, sm, *K2, K2tog, YO; rep from * to last 3 sts, K3.

Rnd 27: Sm, K2tog, YO, K1, YO, ssk, K2tog, YO, K3, YO, ssk, K2tog, YO, K1, YO, ssk, sm, knit to end.

Rnd 29: Sm, K2tog, YO, K1, YO, ssk, K3, YO, ssk, K2, K2tog, YO, K1, YO, ssk, sm, K4, *K2tog, YO, K2; rep from * to last 3 sts, K3.

Rnd 31: Sm, (K2tog, YO, K1, YO, ssk, K1) twice, K2tog, YO, K1, YO, ssk, sm, knit to end.

Rnd 33: Sm, K2tog, YO, K1, YO, ssk, K2tog, YO, K3, YO, ssk, K2tog, YO, K1, YO, ssk, sm, *K2, K2tog, YO; rep from * to last 3 sts, K3.

Rnd 35: Rep rnd 23.

Rnd 37: Sm, (K2tog, YO, K1, YO, ssk, K1) twice, K2tog, YO, K1, YO, ssk, sm, K4, *K2tog, YO, K2; rep from * to last 3 sts, K3.

Rnd 39: Rep rnd 27.

Rnd 41: Sm, K2tog, YO, K1, YO, ssk, K3, YO, ssk, K2, K2tog, YO, K1, YO, ssk, sm, *K2, K2tog, YO; rep from * to last 3 sts, K3.

Rnd 43: Rep rnd 31.

Rnd 45: Sm, K2tog, YO, K1, YO, ssk, K2tog, YO, K3, YO, ssk, K2tog, YO, K1, YO, ssk, K4, *K2tog, YO, K2; rep from * to last 3 sts, K3.

Rnds 46–51: Knit.

Rnd 52: *K2, P2; rep from * to end.

Rnd 53: (K2, P2tog, YO, K2, YO, P2tog) twice, (K2, P2, K2, P2tog, YO, K2, YO, P2tog) 3 times, K2, P2.

Rnds 54–63: Work in K2, P2 ribbing.

Rnds 64–65: Knit.

BO all sts. *Do not* cut yarn. Pick up rem st with size D/3 (3.25 mm) crochet hook and work sl st to finish BO rnd. Finish with scalloped edge as for right sock.

TIES (Make 2)

Measure and cut 128 in. (325 cm) length of yarn; fold it in half. Hold the cut ends in one hand and twist yarn at the loop. When twisted, fold it in half again, still holding the cut ends tog with the loop, and it will automatically twist again. Tie the "loose" ends into a knot. Pull the ties through eyelets and tie into bows.

TIP

When casting on stitches at the toe with needle 2, you can use the smaller size B/1 (2.00 mm) crochet hook to pull the stitches through the spaces between the cast-on stitches, and then put them onto needle 2.

SUGGESTED VARIATIONS

- Make the socks knee-highs for a lingerie look.
- Use store-bought ribbon instead of handmade ties.

DESIGNED BY ELLEN MALLETT

Ribbon Socks

The pretty pink satin ribbon threaded through these cheeky knee socks adds an interesting texture and another color to the design.

YARN

MC: 2 balls of Rowan *4 ply Soft* (100% merino wool; 50 g; 175 m), color 395 Fairy

CC: 1 ball of Rowan *4 ply Soft,* color 394 Dove

NEEDLES

Set of 5 US 2 (2.75 mm) double-pointed needles

EXTRAS

1 yd (90 cm) of pink satin ribbon

Tapestry needle

GAUGE

34 sts and 48 rows = 4 in. (10 cm) in St st on US 2 (2.75 mm) needles

TO FIT

Women's shoe size 6–9

SKILL LEVEL

Intermediate

SOCKS (Make 2)
TOE AND FOOT

Using CC, CO 8 sts on 1 dpn using half-st cast on. Turn needle so bottom loops are on top. Knit first 4 loops onto another dpn and next 4 onto a 3rd dpn. (16 sts)

Knit next 8 sts for front of sock.

Rnd 1
  N1: K1, M1, knit to end of needle.
  N2: Knit to last st, M1, K1.
  N3: K1, M1, knit to last st on needle, M1, K1.

Rnd 2: Knit.

Rep these 2 rnds until there are 60 sts. Change to MC and knit in MC for 6 in. (15 cm).

HEEL

Place 30 sts back on 1 needle and work back and forth:

Row 1: Sl 1, knit across.
Row 2: Sl 1, purl across.

Rep until there are 30 heel-flap rows, ending with a purl row.

Row 1: Sl 1, K15, K2tog, K1, turn.
Row 2: Sl 1, P5, P2tog, P1, turn.
Row 3: Sl 1, K6, K2tog, K1, turn.
Row 4: Sl 1, P7, P2tog, P1, turn.

Rep rows 3 and 4, inc sts worked by 1 each time until all side sts are used, ending with a knit row. (18 sts)

GUSSET

Rnd 1: Using a dpn, pick up and knit 15 sts from side of heel flap plus 1 st in gusset corner, knit across 30 sts on needle at front of sock, pick up and knit 1 st in gusset corner and 15 sts from side of heel flap, knit across 18 sts of sock back. (80 sts on 4 dpns)

LEG

Rnd 1: Knit.

Rnd 2

    N1: Knit to last 2 sts, K2tog.

    N2: Knit.

    N3: Skpo, knit to end of needle.

    N4: Knit. At the same time on next and every following 6th row, work K9, YO, K2tog, knit to end of row.

Cont dec until there are a total of 60 sts. Work in St st with YOs as set until you reach 4¼ in. (11 cm) from first hole.

CALVES

On YO rnds 9, 12, and 15, knit to 1 st before middle of back, M1, K1, YO, K2tog, M1, knit to end. (66 sts)

Cont knitting even, working YOs on every third row until there are 20 YOs up back of sock.

CUFF

Knit in MC to center back—this now becomes end of each rnd.

Move sts onto 3 needles, work 1 rnd of knit in CC.

Work 13 rnds in K1, P1 ribbing.

Using a larger needle, if necessary, BO loosely.

FINISHING

Sew in ends. Lightly block sock. Thread pink satin ribbon through YOs and stitch in place at bottom and top.

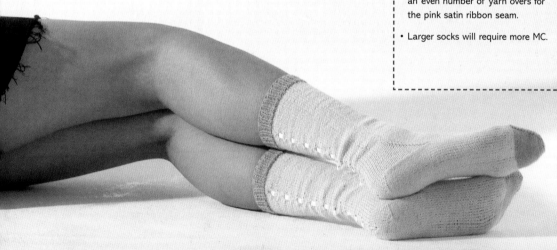

DESIGNED BY P. D. CAGLIASTRO

Circle Socks

Wear these attractive ankle socks with their unusual circle decorations with your heels or with Doc Martins—either way is pretty cool!

YARN

MC: 2 balls of Rowan *4 ply Soft* (100% wool; 50 g; 175 m), color 372 Sooty

A: 1 ball of Rowan *4 ply Soft*, color 380 Marine

B: 1 ball of Rowan *4 ply Soft*, color 387 Rain Cloud

C: 1 ball of Rowan *4 ply Soft*, color 382 Beetroot

D: 1 ball of Rowan *4 ply Soft*, color 374 Honk

NEEDLES

Set of 5 US 3 (3.00 mm) double-pointed needles

EXTRAS

Stitch marker   Yarn needle

Pins

GAUGE

28 sts and 36 rows = 4 in. (10 cm) in St st on US 3 (3.00 mm) needles

TO FIT

Women's shoe size 6–9

SKILL LEVEL

Intermediate

SOCKS (Make 2)

Using C, CO 70 sts. Divide sts as follows:

N1: 17 sts; **N2:** 18 sts; **N3:** 17 sts; **N4:** 18 sts.

Rnd 1: P1, pm, purl to end.

Rnd 2: Knit.

Rnd 3: Join B, *K1 with B; P1 with C, keeping C in front of work, rep from * around.

Rnd 4: *P1 with B, keeping B in front; K1 with C, rep from * around. Drop B.

Rnds 5–9: Cont in K1, P1 ribbing for 5 rnds.

Rnd 10: Knit 1 rnd even.

Rnds 11–12: Change to MC and work 2 rnds even.

DECREASE SECTION

Rnd 13: K33, ssk, K33, K2tog. (68 sts)

Rnd 14: K17, ssk, K32, K2tog, K15. (66 sts)

Rnd 15: K31, ssk, K31, K2tog. (64 sts)

Rnd 16: K15, ssk, K30, K2tog, K15. (62 sts)

Rnd 17: K29, ssk, K29, K2tog. (60 sts)

Work 40 rows even (add rows here to make sock longer).

HEEL FLAP

Knit to 3 sts before marker, join A and work, using intarsia technique, with A behind MC for 3 sts. Drop MC (do not cut) and work on only those 3 sts:

Row 1: K3, turn.

Row 2: P1, K1ftb, purl to end, turn.

Row 3: K1, K1f&b, knit to end, turn.

Rep rows 2 and 3 until there are 19 sts. Work 6 rows even, finishing on a purl row.

Leave these sts on 1 needle.

Return to the sts held in MC. Work in one of these ways:

Simple way:

Working in St st, work 22 rows; sew closed at end.

Advanced way:

Working in St st, pick up edge st of heel flap at *beg* of each row and work it *tog* with first st of each of the 22 rows. Work 1 complete rnd, using intarsia technique to hide MC behind 19 heel sts. K1 into MC.

HEEL TURN

Cont in A:

Turn, P17, P2tog twice.

Turn, sl 1 kw, K17, K2tog twice.

Turn, sl 1 pw, P16, P2tog (from this point on, the 2 sts in this and following row should *always* be 1 of each color).

Turn, sl 1 kw, K16, K2tog.

Rep last 2 rows until total of 52 sts rem.

INSTEP

Drop A; with MC, work 39 rnds even (add or subtract rnds here for size).

Changing colors at st marker, change to A and work 1 rnd even; drop st marker and arrange sts on needles as follows:

N1: 24 sts; **N2:** 2 sts; **N3:** 24 sts; **N4:** 2 sts. (The needles with 2 sts should be on the outer edges of the sock, and the needles with 24 sts should be on the top and bottom of the sock.)

Rnd 1: K2tog at beg and end of N1 and N3 (2 sts will always rem on N2 and N4).

Rnd 2: Knit.

Rep rnds 1 and 2 until 10 sts rem on each of N1 and N3.

K2tog twice at beg and end of N1 and N3. (16 sts)

Work 1 rnd even.

Slide sts from N2 and N4 to closest needles, leaving 8 sts on each of 2 needles. Cut yarn, leaving 10 in. (25 cm); thread yarn through needle and weave sts tog to close toe.

CIRCLES (Make 2 of each color in each size)

LARGE CIRCLE

Using C and leaving a long tail, CO 8 sts. The 8th st will not be used again until BO.

*K7, turn.

P6, turn.

K5, turn.

P4, turn.

K3, turn.

P2, turn.

K2.

Close the circle:

Rep from *4 times more, BO. Leaving a long tail, cut yarn. Steam flat. Thread the yarn needle through the center yarn and weave it around the center opening. Draw the center closed. Sew the 2 edges tog to close the circle. Trim the yarn, but leave the *other* tail to sew circles on.

MEDIUM CIRCLE

Using D and leaving a long tail, CO 7 sts. The 7th st will not be used again until BO.

**K6, turn.
P5, turn.
K4, turn.
P3, turn.
K2, turn.
P2.

Close the circle:

Work as for large circle, working from **.

SMALL CIRCLE

Using A and leaving a long tail, CO 5 sts. The 5th st will not be used again until BO.

***K5, turn.
P4, turn.
K3, turn.
P2, turn.
K2.

Close the circle:

Work as for large circle, working from ***.

FINISHING

Turn sock inside out; pin heel flap to color MC sock areas and sl st closed with the heel-flap color. Steam circles flat. Pin the large circle, aligning it with the lower edge of the ribbing. Pin the medium circle so it touches the bottom edge of the large circle. Pin the small circle so it touches the bottom of the medium circle and meets the top of the heel flap. Whipstitch all circles onto the sock with their remaining tails. Turn sock inside out; tie off and trim excess yarn. Steam the socks after they are completely finished.

TALL TIP

If you want these socks to be taller, add rows as advised in that section.

KNEE SOCKS

For knee socks, increase the length of the ribbing to hold up the weight of the sock and then make additional circles and sew them along the back of the sock.

MAKING YARN SUBSTITUTIONS

For this project, any soft yarn that has the same gauge will do. Wool is recommended rather than cotton. Wool has a "memory" and will hold up the sock under the weight of the added circles.

Crown Slippers

The Goldfingering yarn adds a gleam to these smart black slippers. For extra glamour sew on crystal beads instead of—or in addition to—the sequins!

YARN

MC: 2 balls of Rowan *Pure Wool DK* (100% wool; 50 g; 125 m), color 004 Black
A: 2 balls of Twilleys *Goldfingering* (80% viscose/20% metallized polyester; 50 g; 200 m), color 02 Gold

NEEDLES

US 6 (4.00 mm) knitting needles

EXTRAS

100 multicolored sequins

GAUGE

23 sts and 32 rows = 4 in. (10 cm) in St st on US 6 (4.00 mm) needles

TO FIT

Women's shoe size 6–9

SKILL LEVEL

Advanced

SLIPPERS
ANKLE PIECES (Make 2)
Using MC, CO 80 sts.
Beg at bottom of ankle, work in St st as follows:
Knit 6 rows with MC.
Knit 2 rows with A.
Knit 2 rows with MC.
Next row: Work bobble as follows: K1 with MC; *with A, (K1, P1, K1, P1, K1) into next st, sl second, third, fourth, and fifth sts over first st on needle (1 st in A rem on needle); K3 with MC, rep from * across row to last 3 sts, work bobble in next st, K2, carrying A loosely across back of work.
Purl 1 row with MC.
Beg chart and work until complete, remembering to work last 4 rows in chart as garter st (indicated by "x" in squares).
BO firm (but not tightly).

SOLE (Make 2)
Using A, CO 14 sts.
Row 1: Knit.
Row 2: Purl.
Row 3: K1f&b, knit to last st, K1f&b. (16 sts)
Row 4: Purl.
Rows 5–10: Rep last 2 rows 3 more times. (22 sts)
Rows 11–24: Work in St st.
Row 25: Sl 1, K1, psso, knit to last 2 sts, K2tog. (20 sts)
Rows 26–28: Work in St st.

Row 29: Rep row 25. (18 sts)
Rows 30–40: Work in St st; work should now be 5 in. (12.5 cm).
Row 41: K1f&b, knit to last st, K1f&b. (20 sts)
Row 42: Purl.
Rows 43–48: Rep last 2 rows 3 more times. (26 sts)
Rows 49–70: Work in St st. (26 sts)
Row 71: Sl 1, K1, psso, knit to last 2 sts, K2tog. (24 sts)
Row 72: Purl; work should now be 9 in. (22.5 cm).
Row 73: Sl 1, K1, psso, knit to last 2 sts, K2tog. (22 sts)
Row 74: Purl.
Row 75: Sl 1, K1, psso, knit to last 2 sts, K2tog. (20 sts)

Row 76: P2tog, purl to last 2 sts, P2tog tbl. (18 sts)
Row 77: Sl 1, K1, psso, knit to last 2 sts, K2tog. (16 sts)
Row 78: P2tog, purl to last 2 sts, P2tog tbl. (14 sts)
BO rem 14 sts.

LEFT SIDE OF SLIPPER FOOT
(Make 2 the same)
Using MC, CO 16 sts.
Row 1: Knit.
Row 2: Purl.
Rows 3–32: Cont in St st; work should now be 4 in. (10 cm).
Row 33: K1f&b, knit to end. (17 sts)
Row 34: Purl.
Row 35: Knit.
Row 36: Purl.
Rows 37–44: Rep last 4 rows 2 more times. (19 sts)
Row 45: Knit to last 2 sts, K2tog.
Row 46: Purl.
Row 47: As row 33.
Row 48: Purl.
Row 49: K1f&b, knit to last 2 sts, K2tog.
Rows 50–52: Work in St st.
Row 53: Knit to last 2 sts, K2tog.
Rows 54–56: Work in St st.
Rows 57–68: Rep last 4 rows 3 more times.
Row 69: Knit to last 2 sts, K2tog.
Row 70: Purl.
Rows 71–76: Rep last 2 rows 3 more times.
Row 77: Knit to last 2 sts, K2tog.
Row 78: P2tog, purl to end of row.
Rows 79–84: Rep last 2 rows 3 more times.
BO rem 3 sts.

RIGHT SIDE OF SLIPPER FOOT
(Make 2)
Work as for left side, reversing all shaping.

FINISHING
Sew in ends and press pieces lightly. Sew slipper foot pieces tog along center-front seam, using 1 left and 1 right side; sew along the straight seam from toe to the beg of the shaping. Sew the center-back seam of the slipper-foot pieces. Sew the slipper sole to the bottom edge of the slipper foot. Sew the side seams of each ankle piece tog to make a "cuff." Sew around the bottom edge of the ankle piece, joining it to the slipper foot. Make sure the back seams line up with each other. Decorate with sequins, using photo as a guide for placement.

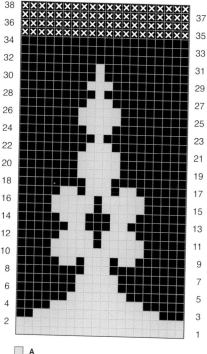

☐ A
■ MC
☒ MC in garter st

TIPS
- When working with yarns MC and A in the same row, weave MC at the back of the work when not in use. Use separate small balls of A for each segment of crown and do not weave across the back.

- To make smaller slippers, use US 3 (4.00 mm) needles. For larger slippers, use US 7 (4.50 mm); this will alter your gauge.

DESIGNED BY TANIS GRAY

Cable Leg Warmers

These chunky cable leg warmers will keep you cozy on even the coldest days. Large needles and chunky yarn mean they knit up quickly, too!

YARN

4 balls of Rowan *Big Wool* (100% merino wool; 100 g; 80 m), color 38 Flirty

NEEDLES	EXTRAS
Set of US 15 (10.00 mm) double-pointed needles	Tapestry needle Cable needle

GAUGE

10 sts and 12 rows = 4 in. (10 cm) in cable pattern on US 15 (10.00 mm) needles

TO FIT	SKILL LEVEL
Women's size Extra Small	Intermediate

SPECIAL ABBREVIATION

LC4: Sl 2 sts to cn and hold to front, K2, K2 from cn.

LEG WARMERS (Make 2)

CO 26 sts, dividing over 3 dpns.

Rnds 1–10: Work 10 rnds in K1, P1 ribbing.

Rnd 11: (K4, P1) to last 2 sts, P2tog. (25 sts)

Rnd 12: (K4, P1) to end.

Rnd 13: Rep rnd 12.

Rnd 14: (LC4, P1) to end.

Rnd 15: Rep rnd 12.

Rnd 16: Rep rnd 12.

Rep rnds 11–16 until 39 rnds of patt have been worked.

Row 50 (cable row): (LC4, P1, inc 1) to end. (30 sts)

Cont knitting rows 11–16, keeping in patt until row 79 is complete; be mindful that row 14 now becomes (LC4, P2) to end.

Row 80 (cable row): (LC4, P2, inc 1) to end. (35 sts)

Knit 3 rnds.

Row 84: (K1, P1) to last 2 sts, P2tog. Cont in ribbing patt for 10 rows total. BO loosely. Weave in all loose ends.

TIPS

- Substitute Debbie Bliss Cashmerino Super Chunky, color 23 Sage (gauge will need to be adjusted slightly).

- Before knitting leg warmers, measure the leg at the ankle, knee, and thigh and adjust pattern accordingly. If your thigh is larger than 14¾ in. (37.5 cm), adjust the size by adding more purl stitches between each cable row.

- Do not bind off too tightly; you don't want the leg warmers to cut off circulation!

- Do not bind off too loosely or the leg warmers will slide right down the leg.

- For a shorter version of the pattern, knit to directly under the knee and bind off, lessening the number of ribbing rows; or add another color and make stripes.

DESIGNED BY SASHA KAGAN

Gypsy Flower Socks

Rediscover flower power with these bright floral socks, which are knitted using the intarsia technique. Remember to twist the yarn when changing color to avoid holes.

YARN

MC: 1 ball of Rowan *Scottish Tweed 4 ply* (100% wool; 25 g; 110 m), color 23 Midnight

A: 3 balls of Rowan *Scottish Tweed 4 ply*, color 05 Lavender

B: 1 ball of Rowan *Scottish Tweed 4 ply*, color 10 Brill Pink

C: 1 ball of Rowan *Scottish Tweed 4 ply*, color 09 Rust

D: 1 ball of Rowan *Scottish Tweed 4 ply*, color 11 Sunset

E: 1 ball of Rowan *Scottish Tweed 4 ply*, color 28 Gold

NEEDLES	**EXTRAS**
US 3 (3.00 mm) knitting needles	Stitch holders
US 2 (2.75 mm) knitting needles	Spare needle

GAUGE

27 sts and 37 rows = 4 in. (10 cm) in St st intarsia patt on US 3 (3.00 mm) needles

---

TO FIT	**SKILL LEVEL**
Women's shoe size 6–9	Intermediate

MOCK CABLE RIB

Row 1: *P2, twist 2 by knitting into second st on LH needle, slightly stretch st just made, knit into back of first st, and sl both sts off needles; rep from * to last 2 sts, P2.
Row 2: (K2, P2) to last 2 sts, K2.
Row 3: (P2, K2) to last 2 sts, P2.
Row 4: As row 2.
These 4 rows form the mock cable rib.

BOBBLE

Knit into back and front of st, turn, K2, turn, P2, turn, K2tog.

SOCKS (Make 2)

Using US 2 (2.75 mm) needles and A, CO 74 sts.
Work row 1 of mock cable rib, beg with P2.
Change to MC and work 2 in. (5 cm) of mock cable rib beg with row 2.
Change to US 3 (3.00 mm) needles and work 26 sts of mock cable rib with MC, K1, work 20 sts of chart, K1, work 26 sts of mock cable rib with MC.
Cont as set until row 48 of chart has been completed.

Divide for heel and instep:

Next row: Cont in patt as set on 55 sts, turn, leaving 19 sts on st holder.
Next row: Cont in patt as set on 36 sts, turn, leaving 19 sts on st holder.
Cont on these 36 sts in patt for 48 rows. Leave these sts on a spare needle.

With RS facing, sl sts from both holders onto 1 needle with back of leg seam at center.
Work 20 rows of mock cable rib.

HEEL TURN

Row 1: K28, skpo, turn.
Row 2: P19, P2tog, turn.
Row 3: K19, skpo, turn.
Row 4: As row 2.
Rep last 2 rows until 20 sts rem, ending with a purl row, then purl
16 sts along side of heel flap onto same needle. (36 sts)
Next row: Knit to end, then knit 16 sts along side of heel flap. (52 sts)
Next row: Purl.

INSTEP SHAPING

Cont in St st.
Row 1: K1, skpo, knit to last 3 sts, K2tog, K1.
Row 2: K1, purl to last st, K1.

Rep last 2 rows until 40 sts rem, then
cont in St st until foot section measures
same as top section, ending with a WS
row.

Next row: Work to end, then work in
St st across 36 sts on spare needle.
(76 sts)

Next row: Purl.

TOE SHAPING

Row 1: (K1, K2tog, K32, K2tog, K1)
twice. (72 sts)

Row 2 and every alt row: Purl.

Row 3: (K1, K2tog, K30, K2tog, K1)
twice. (68 sts)

Row 5: (K1, K2tog, K28, K2tog, K1)
twice. (64 sts)

Cont dec in this way on alternate rows
until a total of 32 sts rem, ending with
a WS row.

Sl first 16 sts onto spare needle, fold
work in half with RS facing, and graft
sts tog.

FINISHING

Tidy loose ends back into their own
color. Join the seams at the side of the
foot and the seam at the back of the
leg. Lightly press only the parts knitted
in St st.

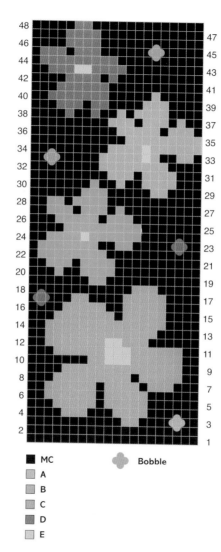

■ MC	Bobble
■ A	
■ B	
■ C	
■ D	
■ E	

DESIGNED BY KATE BUCHANAN

Flip-flop Socks

Get that beach holiday feeling even in the depths of winter! Wear your flip-flops all year around with these snuggly socks that have a separate big toe so your flip-flops fit.

YARN

2 balls of Rowan *Wool Cotton* (50% wool/50% cotton; 50 g; 113 m), color 910 Plum

NEEDLES

Set of 4 US 4 (3.50 mm) double-pointed needles

EXTRAS

Stitch holders
Stitch marker

GAUGE

24 sts and 33 rows = 4 in. (10 cm) in St st on US 4 (3.50 mm) needles

TO FIT

Women's shoe size 6–9

SKILL LEVEL

Intermediate

RIGHT FOOT

CO 52 sts and divide them so there are 16 sts on first needle and 18 sts on the other 2 needles. Join, making sure sts are not twisted, pm to mark beg of rnd. Work K2, P2 ribbing for 2 in. (5 cm). Change to patt:

Rnd 1: Knit.
Rnd 2: *P1, K3; rep from * to end of rnd.
Rnd 3: Knit.
Rnd 4: K2, *P1, K3; rep from * to last 2 sts, P1, K1.
Rep rnds 1–4.

HEEL FLAP

Row 1: Sl 1, K25, turn.
Row 2: Sl 1, P25, turn.
Cont to work on these 26 sts.
Next row: *Sl 1, K1; rep from * to end.
Next row: Sl 1, purl to end.
Rep last 2 rows 13 more times (28 rows in all). Remove marker.

HEEL TURN

Row 1: Sl 1, K15, K2tog, K1, turn.
Row 2: Sl 1, P7, P2tog, P1, turn.
Row 3: Sl 1, K8, K2tog, K1, turn.
Row 4: Sl 1, P9, P2tog, P1, turn.
Row 5: Sl 1, K10, K2tog, K1, turn.
Row 6: Sl 1, P11, P2tog, P1, turn.
Row 7: Sl 1, K12, K2tog, K1, turn.
Row 8: Sl 1, P13, P2tog, P1, turn.
Row 9: Sl 1, K14, K2tog, turn.
Row 10: Sl 1, P14, P2tog, turn. (16 sts)

GUSSET

N1: knit across 16 sts, pick up 15 sts down side edge of heel flap.
N2: Knit next 26 sts.
N3: Pick up 15 sts up other side edge of heel flap, K8 from N1.
Cont as follows:
Rnd 1
   N1: Knit to last 3 sts, K2tog, K1.
   N2: K2, *P1, K3; rep from * to end of needle.
   N3: K1, ssk, knit to end of needle.
Rnd 2: Knit.
Rnd 3
   N1: Knit to last 3 sts, K2tog, K1.
   N2: *P1, K3; rep from * to last 2 sts; P1, K1.
   N3: K1, ssk, knit to end of needle.
Rnd 4: Knit.
Rep rnds 1–4 once more, then repeat rnds 1 and 2 once. (13 sts on needles 1 and 3)

FOOT

Rnd 1: K13, *P1, K3; rep from * to last 2 sts on N2, P1, K1; K13. (52 sts)
Rnd 2: Knit.
Rnd 3: K13, K2, *P1, K3; rep from * to last 2 sts of N2; P1, K1, K13.
Rnd 4: Knit.
Rep rnds 1–4 until sock measures 9 in. (22.5 cm) along sole from heel turn, or work until this measurement is the length of your foot minus 1 in. (2.5 cm). Finish at end of N2.

TOE SHAPING

Work big toe separately as follows:
Next rnd: K7, turn, CO 2 sts, turn, leave next 38 sts on st holder, knit last 7 sts from N2. Distribute these 16 sts onto three needles.
Knit 10 rnds.
Next 2 rnds: *K2tog; rep from * to end of rnd.
Cut yarn and draw end through rem 4 sts.
Join yarn at base of big toe.
Work rest of toes as follows:
   N1: K16, K2tog, K1.
   N2: K1, ssk, K12.
   N3: K4, pick up 2 sts at base of big toe (2 sts CO 2 previously), K4.
Cont to dec as follows:
   N1: Knit to last 3 sts, K2tog, K1.
   N2: K1, ssk, knit to end of needle.
   N3: Knit.
Cont dec in same way on every rnd until 20 sts rem.
Cont to dec as before on N1 and N2 twice more. At the same time, dec on N3 as follows: K1, ssk, knit to last 3 sts, K2tog, K1. (12 sts)
Next rnd: Sl last 3 sts onto new needle, then K3 from N1. On next needle, K3 from N2, then knit last 3 sts from N3. (Sts are now on 2 needles.) Graft sts tog or use 3-needle bind off.

LEFT FOOT

Work as for right foot to toe shaping.

TOE SHAPING

Work big toe separately as follows:

Next rnd: K19, leave these sts on holder, K14, turn, CO 2sts, turn, leave rem 19 sts on st holder. Distribute the 16 sts on 3 needles.

Knit 10 rnds.

Next 2 rnds: *K2tog; rep from * to end of rnd.

Cut yarn and draw end through rem 4 sts. Join yarn at base of big toe.

Work rest of toes as follows:

  N1: K16, K2tog, K1.

  N2: K1, ssk, K12.

  N3: K4, pick up 2 sts at base of big toe (2 sts CO previously), K4.

Cont to dec as follows:

  N1: Knit to last 3 sts, K2tog, K1.

  N2: K1, ssk, knit to end of needle.

  N3: Knit.

Cont dec in same way on every rnd until 20 sts rem.

Cont to dec as before on N1 and N2 twice more. At the same time, dec on N3 as follows: K1, ssk, knit to last 3 sts, K2tog, K1. (12 sts)

Next rnd: Sl last 3 sts onto new needle, K3 from N1. On next needle, K3 from N2, then knit last 3 sts from N3. (Sts are now on 2 needles.)

Graft sts tog or use 3-needle bind off.

FINISHING

Weave in ends. Press lightly as per yarn-label instructions.

DESIGNED BY KAREN GARLINGHOUSE

Slouchy Socks

Snuggle up in these cute "snow bunny" socks! Do just one tier of angora for a shorter sock, or use the angora throughout for a truly decadent bed sock.

YARN

A: 2 balls of Louisa Harding *Kashmir DK* (55% merino wool, 35% microfiber, 10% cashmere; 50 g; 105 m), color 3 Pale Pink or White

B: 3 balls of Louisa Harding *Kimono Angora Pure* (70% angora, 25% wool, 5% nylon; 50 g; 114 m), color 2 Deep Pink

NEEDLES

Set of 4 US 3 (3.00 mm) double-pointed needles
Set of 4 US 2 (2.75 mm) double-pointed needles
US 3 (3.00 mm) 16 in. (40 cm) circular needle
Size G/6 (4.00 mm) crochet hook

GAUGE

24 sts and 36 rows = 4 in. (10 cm) in St st on US 3 (3.0 mm) needles

TO FIT

Women's shoe size 6–9

SKILL LEVEL

Intermediate

SPECIAL ABBREVIATIONS

W&T (wrap and turn): On knit rows, knit specified number of sts. Bring yarn to front of work as if to purl. Slip next st from left needle to right needle. Turn work. Slip first st on right needle back to left needle. Purl next st and across the row. On purl rows, work as for knit rows, except purl the specified number of sts and bring yarn to back of work as if to knit, to wrap the st.

SOCK (Make 2)

FIRST HALF OF TOE

With G/6 (4.00 mm) crochet hook and waste yarn, ch 24. With A and 1 of the US 3 (3.00 mm) dpns, pick up and knit into the center loops of the back side of the chain. Turn and purl back across the sts.

Row 1: K23, W&T.
Row 2: P22, W&T.
Rep rows 1 and 2, dec by 1 st on each row until you have 12 sts and ending on a purl row. You will have 6 wrapped sts on each side of the 12 sts in the middle of the needle. First half of toe is now complete.

SECOND HALF OF TOE

Row 1: K12 to first wrapped st, pick up wrap and knit with next st, turn.
Row 2: Purl to first wrapped st, pick up wrap and purl with next st, turn.
Rep rows 1 and 2 until all wrapped sts are worked. (24 sts)
Your last row will be a purl row.
With 2 dpns, pick up 24 sts from provisional CO. Pull each crochet ch out after you pick up the st. (48 sts)

Beg to work in the rnd:

Rnd 1: Knit even.
Join 2 strands of B, *do not* cut A. Knit 1 row with 2 strands of B; break B, leaving a tail long enough to weave in. Cont with A.
Work even on 48 sts for 6½ in. (16.5 cm) from end of toe. Add or subtract length here for a custom fit.

HEEL

Sl first 24 sts onto 1 needle for instep of sock, cont working heel on rem 24 sts.
Row 1: K23, W&T.
Row 2: P22, W&T.
Rep rows 1 and 2, dec 1 st each row until there are 12 sts left in middle of heel and ending on a purl row (WS). (6 wrapped sts each side, 12 sts in the middle)
Knit across 12 middle sts to first wrapped st, knit wrap and st tog, turn. P13 to first wrapped st on other side, purl wrap and st tog, turn.
Cont until all sts are worked. (24 sts)

GUSSET

Return to working in the rnd with 16 sts on each needle. To avoid having holes at the heel corners, proceed in this manner:
Rnd 1: Knit first 16 sts of heel onto 1 needle. Knit next 8 sts of heel onto a second needle. Pick up 2 sts between second needle and next needle, K8. With third needle, pick up 2 sts between second needle and beg of heel sts, K16. (52 sts)
Rnd 2: K16, K7, K2tog, K9, K16, K2tog. (50 sts)

Rnd 3: K16, K6, K2tog, K9, K15, K2tog. (48 sts)
Knit even on 48 sts until heel is 3 in. (7.5 cm) from bottom of sock. The sock can also be altered to fit at this point.

LEG

Cut A and add 1 strand of B.
Rnds 1–2: Knit even.
Switch to US 3 (3.00 mm) circular needle.
Rnd 3: Knit in the front and back of each st around. (96 sts)
Knit even for 3 in. (7.5 cm) from beg of B.
Next rnd: *K2tog around. (48 sts)
Knit 1 rnd even.
Next rnd: Knit in the front and back of each st around. (96 sts)
Knit even for 3 in. (7.5 cm) from rnd above inc row.**
Rep from * to **. There will be 3 tiers with 2 dec sections.
End with a dec row, then knit even for 2 rnds. (48 sts)
Cut B and join A, switch to US 2 (2.75 mm) dpns on next rnd.
Rnds 1–8: K2, P2 around to create ribbing. Break A and join 2 strands of B.
Rnd 9: Knit even.
Change back to size US 3 (3.00 mm) dpns.
Rnd 10: Knit in the front and back of each st around. (96 sts)
Rnd 11: Knit even.
Rnd 12: Knit in the front and back of each st around. (192 sts)
BO loosely.

DESIGNED BY CLAIRE GARLAND

Lace Anklet Socks

These delicate lacy ankle socks, made in pure silk, are decorated with a pretty daisy motif that has tiny beads added to the "eye" for an extra sparkly touch.

YARN

2 balls of Debbie Bliss *Pure Silk (*100% silk; 50 g; 125 m), color 08 Amethyst

HOOK

Size G/6 (4.00 mm) crochet hook

EXTRAS

6 droplet-style, glass-effect beads   Stitch markers   Yarn needle

GAUGE

20 sts and 22 rnds = 4 in. (10 cm) in sc with G/6 (4.00 mm) hook

TO FIT	SKILL LEVEL
Women's shoe size 6–9	Intermediate/Advanced

SOCKS (Make 2)

TOE

Foundation chain (RS): Ch 4.

Rnd 1: Working over the tail end, work 8 sc in 4th ch from hook, pm to indicate start of rnd.

Rnd 2: *2 sc in each of next sc; rep from * around. (16 sc)

Rnd 3: Rep last rnd. (32 sc)

Rnd 4: 1 sc in each sc around.

Rnd 5: *1 sc in each of next 3 sc, 2 sc in next sc; rep from * 7 more times. (40 sc)

Rnd 6: 1 sc in each sc around.

Rnds 7–14: Rep last rnd 8 more times.

Shape sock sole and sides:

Cont to work in rows along sides and sole of sock.

Row 15: 1 sc in each of next 12 sc, ch 1, turn.

Row 16: 1 sc in each of next 24 sc, ch 1, turn.

Rows 17–31: Rep last row 15 more times.

Row 32: 1 sc in each of next 24 sc; fasten off, ending on a WS row. Cont with heel shaping after completing the square.

DAISY SQUARE

Foundation chain (RS): Ch 5, 1 sl st in first ch made.

Rnd 1: 12 sc into ring, 1 sl st in first sc of rnd.

Rnd 2: (Ch 11, 1 sl st in next sc) 12 times.

Rnd 3: 1 sl st in each of first 6 ch of first ch loop, ch 4, 1 sc in 6th ch of next loop, ch 4, (dc3tog, ch 4, dc3tog) in next loop, *ch 4, (1 dc in 6th ch of next loop, ch 4) twice, (dc3tog, ch 4, dc3tog) in next loop, rep from * twice more, ch 4, 1 sc in same place as 6th sl st at beg of rnd.

Rnd 4: 1 sl st in each of next 2 ch, ch 3, dc2tog in same ch-4 sp, ch 4, 1 sc in next ch-4 sp, ch 4, (dc3tog, ch 4, dc3tog) in ch-4 sp at corner, *ch 4, 1 sc in next ch-4 sp, ch 4, dc3tog in next ch-4 sp, ch 4, 1 sc in next ch-4 sp, ch 4, (dc3tog, ch 4, dc3tog) in ch-4 sp at corner, rep from * twice more, ch 4, 1 sc in next ch-4 sp, ch 4, 1 sl st in third ch of ch-3 at beg of rnd.

Fasten off. Weave in all ends.

Sew daisy square into sock:

With RS of sock facing, ease RS of daisy square against the 3 straight edges of upper sock. Join with small, neat whipstitches. Weave in all ends.

HEEL SHAPING

With RS of sole facing, rejoin yarn to first sc of row 32. Pm**.

Row 33: 1 sc in each of next 24 sc, ch 1, turn.

Rows 34–35: Rep row 33 twice.

Row 36: Ch 1, 1 sc in ch 1, 1 sc in each sc, 2 sc in last sc. (26 sc)

Rows 37–44: Rep rows 33–36 twice. (30 sc)

Row 45: 1 sc in each of next 30 sc, ch 1, turn.

Rep last row twice. Fasten off.

Fold last row (heel end) in half with WS together and join heel seam.

TRIM

Row 1: With RS facing, beg at marker**, join yarn and work 1 row of sc along heel edge, ch 1, turn. (25 sc)

Row 2: 1 sc in each sc across, turn.

Row 3: *Sk 1 sc, 5 dc in next sc, sk 1 sc, 1 sc in next sc; rep from *, ending with 1 sc in last sc.

Fasten off. Weave in ends.

Sew 3 beads onto flower center.

TIP

Make pairs in several colors to match all your pajamas! Or make 1 set in multicolored yarn that will go with everything.

DESIGNED BY MALGOSIA DZIK-HOLDEN

Silk Hose

Pure silk gives a luxurious feel to these supersoft knitted stockings, and the bright, jewel-like colors will add a great look to any outfit.

YARN

MC: 5 balls of Debbie Bliss *Pure Silk* (100% silk; 50 g; 125 m), color 07 Aqua

CC: 2 balls of Debbie Bliss *Pure Silk,* color 12 Coral

NEEDLES

Set of 5 US 0 (2.00 mm) double-pointed needles

GAUGE

28 sts and 38 rows = 4 in. (10 cm) in St st on US 0 (2.00 mm) needles

TO FIT

Women's shoe size 6–9

SKILL LEVEL

Intermediate/Advanced

STOCKINGS (Make 2)
LEG
Using 1 strand each of MC and CC held tog and long-tail method, CO 80 sts onto 1 needle. Divide sts evenly between 4 needles and join for working in the rnd, being careful not to twist sts. Pm after first st to denote beg of rnd. Cut CC, work to end with 1 strand of MC. Knit 1 rnd.

CUFF
Rnd 1: *K2, P2; rep from * to end. Rep this rnd 19 more times; work measures about 2 in. (5 cm) from beg.
Begin faggoted patt:
(Multiple of 20 sts)

Rnds 1, 3, and 5: *P4, (K1 tbl, K1) twice, (YO, P2tog) 4 times, (K1, K1 tbl) twice; rep from * to end.
Rnds 2, 4, and 6: *P4, (K1 tbl, P1) twice, (K2tog, YO) 4 times, (P1, K1 tbl) twice; rep from * to end.
Rnds 7, 9, and 11: *P4, K1 tbl, K1, K1 tbl, K10, K1 tbl, K1, K1 tbl; rep from * to end.
Rnds 8, 10, and 12: *P4, (K1 tbl, P1) twice, K8, (P1, K1 tbl) twice; rep from * to end.
Rep rnds 1–12 a total of 2 times and rnds 1–6 once.
Rnd 31: Knit to last 14 sts, K1 tbl, K1, (YO, P2tog) 4 times, K1, K1 tbl, K2.
Rnd 32: Knit to last 14 sts, K1 tbl, P1, (K2tog, YO) 4 times, P1, K1 tbl, K2.

Rep the last 2 rnds a total of 5 times, then rnd 31 once; work measures about 6 in. (15 cm) from CO.
Inc rnd: K1, M1, knit to last 17 sts, M1, K3, K1 tbl, P1, (K2tog, YO) 4 times, P1, K1 tbl, K2. (2 sts inc, 82 sts) Work 4 rnds even.
Next rnd: Knit to last 14 sts, K1 tbl, K1, (YO, P2tog) 4 times, K1, K1 tbl, K2.
Next rnd: Knit to last 14 sts, K1 tbl, P1, (K2tog, YO) 4 times, P1, K1 tbl, K2. Rep the last 2 rnds once.
Inc rnd: K1, M1, knit to last 17 sts, M1, K3, K1 tbl, K1, (YO, P2tog) 4 times, K1, K1 tbl, K2. (2 sts inc, 84 sts) Work 4 rnds even.
Next rnd: Knit to last 14 sts, K1 tbl, P1, (K2tog, YO) 4 times, P1, K1 tbl, K2.
Next rnd: Knit to last 14 sts, K1 tbl, K1, (YO, P2tog) 4 times, K1, K1 tbl, K2. Rep the last 2 rnds once.

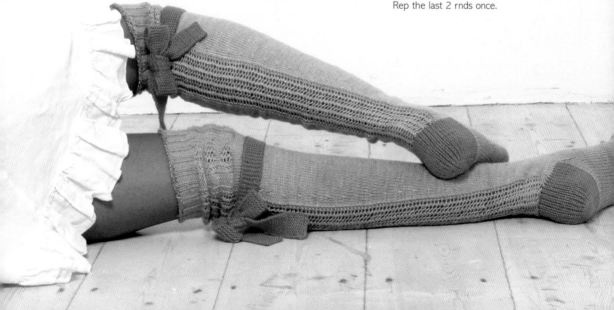

Inc rnd: K1, M1, knit to last 17 sts, M1, K3, K1 tbl, P1, (K2tog, YO) 4 times, P1, K1 tbl, K2. (2 sts inc, 86 sts) Work 7 rnds even; work should measure 7¾ in. (19.5 cm) from CO.

Dec rnd: K2tog, knit to last 18 sts, skpo, K2, K1 tbl, P1, (K2tog, YO) 4 times, P1, K1 tbl, K2. (2 sts dec, 84 sts) Work 7 rnds even.

Rep the last 8 rnds 17 more times. (50 sts)

Work 6 rnds even. Work should measure about 22 in. (56 cm) from CO.

Next rnd: Knit.

Next rnd: Knit to last 21 sts of rnd.

HEEL FLAP

Place next 26 sts (unworked 21 sts from end of this rnd and first 5 sts of this rnd on other side of faggoted section), onto 1 needle to work for heel; 12 sts of faggoted section [K1 tbl, P1, (K2tog, YO) 4 times, P1, K1 tbl] should be situated in center of heel needle, with 7 sts added on each side, equals 26 sts. Place rem 24 sts on 2 needles to be worked later for instep.

Cut MC. The heel is worked in 2 strands of CC to add extra padding and reinforce the heel.

Work 26 heel sts back and forth in rows as follows:

Row 1 (RS): Sl 1, K25.

Row 2 (WS): Sl 1, P25.

Rep rows 1 and 2 until a total of 26 rows have been worked, ending with a WS row. (13 chain sts along each edge of heel flap)

HEEL TURN

Work short rows as follows:

Row 1 (RS): Sl 1, K13, K2tog, turn.

Row 2 (WS): Sl 1, P2, P2tog, turn.

Row 3: Sl 1, K2, K2tog, turn.

Row 4: Sl 1, P2, P2tog, turn.

Rep rows 3 and 4 until all heel sts have been worked. (4 heel sts rem)

Cut off both threads of CC, leaving enough length to weave in later.

GUSSET

Rejoin MC for working in the rnd as follows:

Rnd 1

  N1: Pick up 13 sts along side of heel flap, then work 2 sts of heel.

  N2: Work 2 rem sts of heel, then pick up 13 sts along other side of heel flap.

  N3: Work first 12 sts of instep.

  N4: Work rem 12 sts of instep. (total of 54 sts)

Rnd begins at side of heel.

Rnd 2: Knit to last st on N4, transfer last st onto N1.

Rnd 3

  N1: Sl 1, K1, psso, knit to end (note that last st from N4 now rem on N1).

  N2: Knit to last st, transfer this st to N3.

  N3: K2tog, knit to end.

  N4: Knit all sts. (2 sts dec, total of 52 sts)

Rnd 4: Knit to end of rnd.

Rnd 5

  N1: Skpo, knit to end.

  N2: Knit to last st, transfer this st to N3.

  N3: K2tog, knit to end.

  N4: Knit all sts. (2 sts dec, total of 50 sts)

Pm between first and second st on N1.

FOOT

Work even in St st until foot measures 7 in. (17.5 cm) from back of heel or 2½ in. (6.5 cm) less than desired total length.

To preserve the symmetry between underside and upper side of foot section, sl first st on N1 back onto N4; once this is done, you should have 25 sts in total on N1 and N2, and 25 sts total on N3 and N4.

To prepare for working toe, knit to end of N1. Cut MC, leaving a 12 in. (30.5 cm) tail. From now on, rnd beg at back of heel.

TOE

Switch to 2 strands of CC.

Rnd 1: Knit to end. When working first rnd of toe, pm between first and second st on needle where color was switched, which will be referred to as N1 from now on. References for all other needles change accordingly.

Rnd 2

  N1: Knit to last 3 sts, K2tog, K1.

  N2: K1, skpo, knit to end.

  N3: Knit to last 3 sts, K2tog, K1.

  N4: K1, skpo, knit to end. (4 sts dec, total 46 sts)

Rep rnds 1 and 2 another 8 times. (14 sts)

Next rnd: Work as rnd 2. (10 sts) Cut yarn, leaving 12 in. (30.5 cm) tail.

FINISHING
Thread tail on a tapestry needle, draw through rem sts, and pull up snugly to close end of toe. Weave in loose ends. Block on sock blockers or under a damp towel.

GARTERS (Make 2)
With C, CO 9 sts. Work garter st (knit every row) until work measures 27½ in. (70 cm) from beg. BO all sts. Weave in loose ends.

TIPS
- Try Rowan 4 ply Soft for a more basic and warmer version. You will need to double-check your gauge.

- It's helpful to take note of the faggoted-panel sequence and have it at hand for reference until you memorize it.

- This pattern can be made in plain stockinette stitch with a K2, P2 ribbed cuff instead of a decorative faggoted section. This is especially advised for adventurous beginners who would like to learn how to make stockings without the added difficulty of working a complex lace pattern.

Diamond Slippers

These smart slippers are ideal for lazy evenings at home. If you don't want to knit the beads in as you work, sew them on afterward.

YARN

MC: 2 balls of Rowan *Kid Classic* (70% lambs wool, 26% kid mohair, 4% nylon, 50 g; 114 m), color 831 Smoke

A: 2 balls of Debbie Bliss *Donegal Aran Tweed* (100% wool; 50 g; 88 m), color 03 Dark Brown

B: 1 ball of Debbie Bliss *Donegal Aran Tweed*, color 04 Beige

---

NEEDLES	EXTRAS
US 8 (5.00 mm) knitting needles	150 multicolored plastic or wood beads
US 7 (4.50 mm) knitting needles	with large holes

GAUGE
---

18 sts and 24 rows = 4 in. (10 cm) in St st on US 8 (5.00 mm) needles

---

TO FIT	SKILL LEVEL
Women's shoe size 6–9	Intermediate

SLIPPERS

ANKLE PIECES (Make 2)

Using US 7 (4.50 mm) needles and MC, CO 48 sts and work in K2, P2 ribbing for 15 rows.
Change to US 8 (5.00 mm) needles.
Knit 2 rows with B.
Join A, knit 8 rows.
Join B, knit 2 rows.
Knit 8 rows with MC.
*Break MC and thread on 24 beads.
With WS facing and MC, knit and add a bead in between every alternate st.
Work 14 rows of chart in St st.
Knit 1 row with MC.
Break MC and thread on 24 beads.
With WS facing and MC, knit and add a bead in between every alt st.
Knit 3 rows with MC.
Thread 24 beads onto MC.
With WS facing and MC, knit and add a bead in between every alternate st.
Knit 4 rows with MC.
BO with MC.

SLIPPER SOLE (Make 2)

Using A and size US 7 (4.50 mm) needles, CO 6 sts.
Row 1: Knit.
Row 2: Purl.
Row 3: CO 4 sts kw at beg of row, knit to end. (10 sts)
Row 4: CO 4 sts pw at beg of row, purl to end. (14 sts)
Row 5: CO 2 sts kw at beg of row, knit to end. (16 sts)
Row 6: CO 2 sts pw at beg of row, purl to end. (18 sts)
Rows 7–14: Work in St st.
Cont in St st, dec 1 st at each end of next 3 rows. (12 sts)
Work 4 rows in St st.
Cont in St st, inc 1 st at beg of next 8 rows. (20 sts)
Work even in St st until sole measures 9 in. (22.5 cm) long.
Cont in St st, dec 1 st at end of every row until 14 sts rem.
Cont in St st, dec 2 sts at each end of every row until 6 sts rem.
BO.

LEFT SIDE OF SLIPPER FOOT (Make 2)

Using US 8 (5.00 mm) needles and MC, CO 4 sts and work in St st as follows:
Row 1: Purl with MC.
Row 2: With RS facing, CO 4 sts, knit to end. (8 sts)
Row 3: Purl.
Row 4: CO 2 sts, knit to end. (10 sts)
Row 5: Purl.

Inc 1 st on same side (beg RS row and end of WS) row until you have total of 22 sts.
With WS facing, dec 1 st at beg of next and alternate rows until there are 18 sts.
Work even in St st until piece measures 8 in. (20 cm) long.
With WS facing, inc 1 st at beg of alternate rows until there are 21 sts.
With RS facing, dec 1 st at beg of next and alternate rows until there are 18 sts.
BO 2 sts at beg of next 5 rows. (8 sts)
BO rem 8 sts.

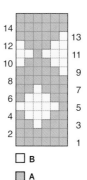

☐ B

▨ A

RIGHT SIDE OF SLIPPER FOOT (Make 2)

Work as for left side, but reverse all shaping.

FINISHING

Sew in ends and press pieces lightly. Sew the foot pieces tog along the center-front seam, using 1 left and 1 right side; sew along the straight seam from the toe to the beg of the shaping. Sew the center-back seam of the foot pieces. Sew the slipper sole to the bottom edge of the slipper foot. Sew the side seams of each ankle piece tog to make a cuff. Sew around the bottom edge of the ankle piece, joining it to the slipper foot. Make sure the back seams line up with each other.
Embroider bottom foot seam with blanket stitch.

POM-POMS (Make 2)

Cut 2 circles from cardboard, then cut smaller circles out of the center of each. Place the card circles tog and using MC and B, wind yarn around the card and through the central hole until they are well covered. Slide the blade of a pair of scissors between the card circles and carefully cut around between the 2 pieces. Pull the pieces of card apart slightly and tie a length of yarn around the center of the pom-pom to secure. Remove the card circles, fluff up the pom-pom, and trim it even. Sew 1 pom-pom onto the front of each slipper.

DESIGNED BY SIÂN LUYKEN

Kilt Socks

These kilt socks are very versatile, and the pattern could be knitted in any Aran-weight yarn. Why not make a pair in cotton for the summer?

YARN

2 balls of Rowan *Scottish Tweed Aran* (100% wool; 100 g; 170 m), color 021 Winter Navy

NEEDLES

US 8 (5.00 mm) knitting needles
Set of 4 US 8 (5.00 mm) double-pointed needles
US 10½ (6.5 mm) knitting needles

EXTRAS

Stitch marker   Darning needle

GAUGE

20 sts and 28 rows = 4 in. (10 cm) in St st on US 8 (5 mm) needles

TO FIT   SKILL LEVEL

Women's shoe size 6–9   Intermediate

SPECIAL ABBREVIATIONS

P2left: Purl into back of second st, purl into back of first st, slip both sts off needle. (The back of the st is understood to be on the inside of the sock.)

P2right: Purl into front of second st, purl into front of first st, slip both sts off needle. (The front of the st is understood to be the side nearest you, on the outside of the sock.)

SOCKS (Make 2)

TOE

Using US 8 (5.00 mm) needles and waste yarn, CO 16 sts and work 2 rows in St st.

Start working in the project yarn.

Next row: P15, take yarn back as if to knit and sl next st, turn, take yarn back to knit and sl st back creating a wrap around base of unworked st.

Next row: K14, bring yarn forward as if to purl and sl next st, turn, bring yarn forward to purl and sl st back.

Cont in this way, working 1 less st on every row until 6 sts rem.

Next row: P6, sl next st onto RH needle, pick up wrap with LH needle, pass slipped st back. Insert tip of RH needle into st and wrap as if to knit, sl them off LH needle. Now insert LH needle through st and wrap so RH needle is ready to purl. Purl st and wrap tog, take yarn back as if to knit and sl next st, turn, take yarn back to knit and sl st back creating a wrap around base of unworked st.

Next row: K7, sl next st onto RH needle, pick up wrap with LH needle, pass slipped st back. Insert tip of RH needle into st and wrap as if to purl, sl off LH needle. Now insert LH needle through st and wrap so RH needle is ready to knit. Knit wrap and st tog, bring yarn forward as if to purl and sl next st, turn, bring yarn forward to purl and sl st back. Cont working 1 st more on each row until all sts are live.

FOOT

Divide sts evenly over 2 needles. Carefully unpick waste yarn and place sts from provisional CO onto a 3rd needle. Pm between first and second st in on this needle to mark beg of rnd. Knit 50 rnds.

HEEL SHAPING

Next rnd: K16, wrap next st and turn work. Remove st marker. Work back and forth as you did for the toe, knitting 1 less st every row until 6 sts rem, turn, P6, pick up next st as explained above. Cont in this way until all sts are live again.

LEG

Replace st marker at beg of rnd and place a different-colored marker after 8th st.

Knit 1 rnd.

Next rnd: Knit into st below 9th st and then into 9th st itself. Cont working in the rnd, inc into the st after the 2nd st marker every 10th rnd until you have 45 sts.

CUFF

Rnds 1–15: *K2, P2, K2, P2, K3, P2, K2; rep from * to end.

Rnd 16: *K2, P2left, K2, P2left, K3, P2, K2; rep from * to end.

Rnd 17: As rnd 1.

Rnd 18: As rnd 16.

Rnd 19: *K1 (P2left, P2right) twice, K2, P2, K2; rep from * to end.

Rnd 20: *K1, P1, K2, P2, K2, P1, K2, P2, K2; rep from * to end.

Rnd 21: *K1, P1, K2, K2left, K2, P1, K2, P2, K2; rep from * to end.

Rnd 22: As rnd 20.
Rnd 23: *K1 (P2right, P2left) twice, K2,
P2, K2; rep from * to end.
Rnd 24: As rnd 1.
Rnd 25: *K2, P2right, K2, P2right, K3,
P2, K2; rep from * to end.
Rnd 26: As rnd 1.
Rnd 27: As rnd 25.
Rnds 28–40: As rnd 1.
BO very loosely using a
US 10½ (6.5 mm) needle.

FINISHING

Weave in all ends and block.

Basic Techniques

Knitting

GAUGE AND SELECTING CORRECT NEEDLE SIZE

Gauge can differ quite dramatically between knitters. This is because of the way that the needles and the yarn are held. So if your gauge does not match that stated in the pattern, you should change your needle size following this simple rule:

- If your knitting is too loose, your gauge will read that you have fewer stitches and rows than the given gauge, and you will need to change to a smaller needle to make the stitch size smaller.
- If your knitting is too tight, your gauge will read that you have more stitches and rows than the given gauge, and you will need to change to a thicker needle to make the stitch size bigger.

Please note that if the projects in this book are not knitted to the correct gauge, yarn quantities will be affected.

KNITTING A GAUGE SWATCH

No matter how excited you are about a new knitting project, take the time to knit a gauge swatch for accurate sizing. Use the same needles, yarn, and stitch pattern that will be used for the main work and knit a sample at least 5 in. (12.5 cm) square. Smooth out the finished piece on a flat surface, but do not stretch it.

To check the stitch gauge, place a ruler horizontally on the sample, measure 4 in. (10 cm) across, and mark with a pin at each end. Count the number of stitches between the pins. To check the row gauge, place a ruler vertically on the sample, measure 4 in. (10 cm), and mark with pins. Count the number of rows between the pins. If the number of stitches and rows is greater then specified in the pattern, make a new swatch using larger needles; if it is less, make a new swatch using smaller needles.

MAKING A SLIPKNOT

A slipknot is the basis of all casting-on techniques and is therefore the starting point for almost everything you do in knitting and crochet.

1
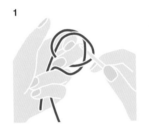
1 Wind the yarn around two fingers twice as shown. Insert a knitting needle through the first (front) strand and under the second (back) one.

2
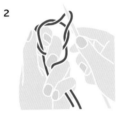
2 Using the needle, pull the back strand through the front one to form a loop.

3

3 Holding the loose ends of the yarn with your left hand, pull the needle upward, tightening the knot. Pull the ball end of the yarn again to tighten the knot further.

CASTING ON

"Casting on" is the term used for making a row of stitches to be used as a foundation for your knitting.

1

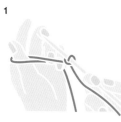

1 Make a slipknot 40 in. (100 cm) from the end of the yarn. Hold the needle in your right hand with the ball end of the yarn over your right index finger. *Wind the loose end of the yarn around your left thumb from front to back.

2

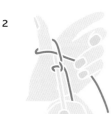

2 Insert the point of the needle under the first strand of yarn on your thumb.

3 With your right index finger, take the ball end of the yarn over the point of the needle.

3

4 Pull a loop through to form the first stitch. Remove your left thumb from the yarn. Pull the loose end to secure the stitch. Repeat from * until the required number of stitches have been cast on.

4

THE BASIC STITCHES

The knit and purl stitches form the basis of all knitted fabrics. The knit stitch is the easiest to learn and once you have mastered this, you can move on to the purl stitch, which is the reverse of the knit stitch.

KNIT STITCH

1

1 Hold the needle with the cast-on stitches in your left hand, with the loose yarn at the back of the work. Insert the right-hand needle from left to right through the front of the first stitch on the left-hand needle.

2

2 Wrap the yarn from left to right over the point of the right-hand needle.

3 Draw the yarn through the stitch, thus forming a new stitch on the right-hand needle.

3

4 Slip the original stitch off the left-hand needle, keeping the new stitch on the right-hand needle.

5 To knit a row, repeat steps 1 to 4 until all the stitches have been transferred from the left-hand needle to the right-hand needle. Turn the work, transferring the needle with the stitches to your left hand to work the next row.

4

PURL STITCH

1

2

3

4

1 Hold the needle with the stitches in your left hand, with the loose yarn at the front of the work. Insert the right-hand needle from right to left into the front of the first stitch on the left-hand needle.

2 Wrap the yarn from right to left, up and over the point of the right-hand needle.

3 Draw the yarn through the stitch, thus forming a new stitch on the right-hand needle.

4 Slip the original stitch off the left-hand needle, keeping the new stitch on the right-hand needle.

5 To purl a row, repeat steps 1 to 4 until all the stitches have been transferred from the left-hand needle to the right-hand needle. Turn the work, transferring the needle with the stitches to your left hand to work the next row.

INCREASING AND DECREASING

Many projects will require some shaping, either to add interest or to allow them to fit comfortably. Shaping is achieved by increasing or decreasing the number of stitches you are working.

INCREASING

The simplest method of increasing one stitch is to work into the front and back of the same stitch.

On a knit row, knit into the front of the stitch to be increased into; then before slipping it off the needle, place the right-hand needle behind the left-hand one and knit again into the back of it (inc). Slip the original stitch off the left-hand needle. On a purl row, purl into the front of the stitch to be increased into; then before slipping it off the needle, purl again into the back of it. Slip the original stitch off the left-hand needle.

DECREASING

The simplest method of decreasing one stitch is to work two stitches together.

On a knit row, insert the right-hand needle from left to right through *two* stitches instead of one; then knit them together as one stitch. This is called knit two together (K2tog).

On a purl row, insert the right-hand needle from right to left through *two* stitches instead of one; then purl them together as one stitch. This is called purl two together (P2tog).

- -

INTARSIA STITCHES

"Intarsia" is the name given to color knitting where the pattern is worked in large blocks of color at a time, requiring a separate ball of yarn for each area of color.

DIAGONAL COLOR CHANGE WITH A SLANT TO THE LEFT	DIAGONAL COLOR CHANGE WITH A SLANT TO THE RIGHT	VERTICAL COLOR CHANGE

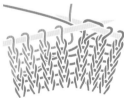

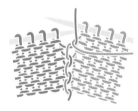

On a wrong-side row, with the yarns at the front of the work, take the first color over the second color, drop it, and then pick up the second color underneath the first color, thus crossing the two colors together.

On a right-side row, with the yarns at the back of the work, take the first color over the second color, drop it, and then pick up the second color underneath the first color, thus crossing the two colors.

Work in the first color to the color change; then drop the first color and pick up the second color underneath the first color, crossing the two colors over before working the next stitch in the second color. Work the first stitch after a color change firmly to avoid a gap forming between colors.

FAIR ISLE STITCHES

Stranding is used when the yarn not in use is left at the back of the work until needed. The loops formed by this are called "floats," and it is important that they are not pulled too tightly when working the next stitch; this will pull in your knitting.

1  **2**  **3** 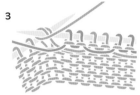 **4**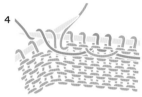

1 On a knit row, hold the first color in your right hand and the second color in your left hand. Knit the required number of stitches as usual with the first color, carrying the second color loosely across the wrong side of the work.

2 To knit a stitch in the second color, insert the right-hand needle into the next stitch, and then draw a loop through from the yarn held in the left hand, carrying the yarn in the right hand loosely across the wrong side until required.

3 On a purl row, hold the yarns as for the knit rows. Purl the required number of stitches as usual with the first color, carrying the second color loosely across these stitches on the wrong side of the work.

4 To purl a stitch in the second color, insert the right-hand needle into the next stitch, and then draw a loop through from the yarn held in the left hand, carrying the yarn in the right hand loosely across the wrong side until required.

BINDING OFF

This is the most commonly used method of securing stitches at the end of a piece of knitting. The bind-off edge should have the same "give" or elasticity as the fabric; bind off in the stitch used for the main fabric unless the pattern directs otherwise.

KNITWISE

Knit two stitches. *Using the point of the left-hand needle, lift the first stitch on the right-hand needle over the second; then drop it off the needle. Knit the next stitch and repeat from * until all stitches have been worked off the left-hand needle and only one stitch remains on the right-hand needle. Cut the yarn, leaving enough to sew in the end, thread the end through the stitch, and then slip it off the needle. Draw the yarn up firmly to fasten off.

PURLWISE

Purl two stitches. *Using the point of the left-hand needle, lift the first stitch on the right-hand needle over the second and drop it off the needle. Purl the next stitch and repeat from * until all the stitches have been worked off the left-hand needle and only one stitch remains on the right-hand needle. Cut the yarn, leaving enough to sew in the end, thread the end through the stitch, and then slip it off the needle. Draw the yarn up firmly to fasten off.

Crochet

GAUGE

This is the number of rows and stitches per inch or centimeter, usually measured over a 4 in. (10 cm) square. The gauge will determine the size of the finished item. The correct gauge is given at the beginning of each pattern. Crochet a small swatch using the recommended yarn and hook to make sure you are working to the correct gauge. If your work is too loose, choose a hook that is one size smaller, and if it is too tight, choose a hook the next size up. When making clothes, it is important to check your gauge before you start; it is not worth making something the wrong size. When measuring your work, lay it on a flat surface and always measure at the center rather than the side edges.

BASIC STITCHES

Start by making a series of chains—around 10 will be enough. Now you're ready to practice the following stitches.

SLIP STITCH (SL ST)

1

This is the shortest stitch, mostly used for joining and shaping. Insert the hook into a stitch or chain (always remember to insert the hook under both strands of the stitch), yarn over the hook from the back to the front of the hook, and draw the hook through the stitch and the loop on the hook. You are left with just 1 loop on the hook. This is 1 slip stitch.

SINGLE CROCHET (SC)

1   2

1 Insert the hook into the second chain from the hook, yarn over the hook, and draw the loop through your work.

2 Yarn over and draw the hook through both loops on the hook; 1 loop on the hook. This is 1 single crochet.

3 Repeat into the next stitch or chain until you've reached the end of the row. Make 1 chain stitch—this is your turning chain— turn the work, and work 1 single crochet into each stitch of the previous row, ensuring you insert the hook under both loops of the stitch you are crocheting into.

HALF DOUBLE CROCHET (HDC)

1

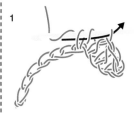

2 When you reach the end of the row, make 2 chains—this counts as the first stitch of the next row. Turn the work, skip the first half double crochet of the previous row, and insert the hook into the second stitch of the new row. Continue to work until the end of the row. At the end of the row, work the last half double crochet into the top of the turning chain of the row below.

1 Yarn over the hook before inserting the hook into the third chain from the hook, yarn over, draw 1 loop through the work, yarn over, draw through all 3 loops on the hook; 1 loop on the hook. This is 1 half double crochet.

DOUBLE CROCHET (DC)

1 Start by wrapping the yarn over the hook and insert the hook into the fourth chain from the hook, yarn over, draw 1 loop through the work.

2 Yarn over, draw through the first 2 loops on the hook, yarn over, draw through the remaining 2 loops on the hook; 1 loop on the hook. This is 1 double crochet.

3 When you reach the end of the row, make 3 chains. These count as the first stitch of the next row. Turn the work and skip the first double crochet of the previous row; insert the hook into the second stitch of the new row. Continue to work until the end of the row, inserting the last double crochet into the top of the turning chain of the row below.

1

2

BASIC TECHNIQUES

As well as working from right to left in rows, crochet can also be worked in a circular fashion (referred to as working in the round), or even in a continuous spiral to make seamless items such as hats, bags, and other rounded objects.

MAKING FABRIC—WORKING IN ROWS

1

Make as many chain stitches as you require. This row is called the base chain. Insert the hook into the second chain from the hook (not counting the chain on the hook) for single crochet or the third chain from the hook for double crochet (fig. 1).

2
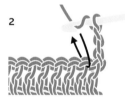

Work from right to left, inserting the hook under 2 of the 3 threads in each chain.

When you reach the end of the row, work one or more turning chains, depending on the height of the stitch.

3
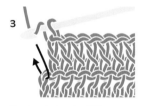

Turning chains should be worked as follows:
Single crochet: 1 chain
Half double: 2 chains
Double: 3 chains
Treble: 4 chains

Now turn the work to begin working on the next row (remember to always turn your work in the same direction). When working in single crochet, insert the hook into the first stitch in the new row and work each stitch to the end of the row, excluding the turning chain. For all other stitches, unless the pattern states otherwise, the turning chain counts as the first stitch; skip 1 stitch (fig. 2), and work each stitch to the end of the row, including the top of the turning chain (fig. 3).

MAKING FABRIC—WORKING IN THE ROUND

1

2

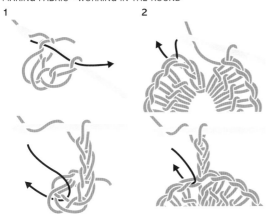

1 Crochet in the round starts with a ring. To make a ring, make a series of chains and join the last chain to the first with a slip stitch.

2 To make the first round, work a starting chain to the height of the stitch you are working in. Then work as many stitches as you need into the center of the ring and finish the round with a slip stitch into the first stitch.

3 Begin the second and subsequent rounds with a starting chain (worked the same way as a turning chain, with the number of chains depending on the stitch you are working; see page 92). Then insert the hook under the top 2 loops of each stitch in the previous round. At the end of the round, join to the top of the starting chain with a slip stitch as in step 2.

INCREASING

As with knitting, fabric is often shaped by increasing the number of stitches in a row or round. To increase, simply work an additional stitch into the next stitch. A single increase is made by working 2 stitches into the same stitch. You can increase by more than 1 stitch at a time.

DECREASING

SC2TOG

To decrease 1 stitch in single crochet (sc2tog), insert the hook into the next stitch, yarn over, draw through the work, insert the hook into the next stitch, yarn over, draw through the work, yarn over, and draw through all 3 loops, leaving just 1 loop on the hook.

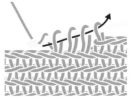

SC3TOG

To decrease by 2 stitches in single crochet, work 3 stitches together (sc3tog) by working as for sc2tog until you have 3 loops on the hook, insert the hook into the next stitch, yarn over, draw through the work, yarn over, and draw through all 4 loops.

DC2TOG

To decrease 1 stitch in double crochet (dc2tog), yarn over, insert hook into next stitch, yarn over, draw through work, yarn over, draw through 2 loops, yarn over, insert hook into next stitch, yarn over, draw through work, yarn over, draw through 2 loops, yarn over, and draw through all 3 loops.

FASTENING OFF AND SEAMS

Once your work is fastened off, there are various ways of sewing up seams. Two principal methods are given here: joining the seams edge to edge using overcast stitch, and slip-stitching seams.

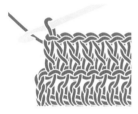
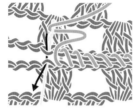

FASTENING OFF

Cut the yarn, leaving roughly 5 in. (13 cm). Make 1 chain, draw the tail through the chain, and pull firmly. Weave the end an inch or a few centimeters in one direction, and then back the other way for a neat and secure finish.

OVERCAST STITCH

This seam creates an almost invisible join. Lay the 2 sections right side up with the stitches aligned. Insert a tapestry needle under the lower half of the edge stitch on one section, and then under the upper half of the edge stitch on the opposite section.

SLIP STITCH

With right sides together, insert the hook into the first stitch of both sections, yarn over the hook, and draw the loop through both stitches and the loop on the hook. Repeat along the length of the seam.

Abbreviations and Glossary

KNITTING ABBREVIATIONS

approx = approximately

beg = beginning

CC = contrasting color

cn = cable needle

CO = cast on

cont = continue

dec = decrease

dpn = double-pointed needles

inc = increase/increasing

K= knit

K2tog = knit 2 stitches together

LH = left hand

M1 = Make 1 stitch. Lift the horizontal strand between the stitch just worked and next stitch; then knit through back of this thread.

MC = main color

P = purl

P2tog = purl 2 stitches together

patt = pattern

pm = place marker

psso = pass slipped stitch over

rem = remaining

rep = repeat

RH = right hand

rnd = round

RS = right side

sl = slip

sm = slip marker

skpo = slip 1 stitch knitwise, knit 1 stitch, pass slipped stitch over

ssk = slip 1 stitch knitwise, slip 1 stitch knitwise, knit 2 stitches together

St st = stockinette stitch

st(s) = stitch(es)

tog = together

TS = thumb section

tbl = through back of loops

WS = wrong side

YO = yarn over needle

CROCHET ABBREVIATIONS

ch = chain

dc = double crochet

dc2tog = double crochet two together

dc3tog = double crochet three together

hdc = half double crochet

sc = single crochet

sc2tog = single crochet two together

sl st = slip stitch

YO = yarn over

KITCHENER STITCH

With the stitches on two parallel, double-pointed needles, make sure that the working yarn is coming from the back needle. Take the tapestry needle through the first stitch on the front needle as if to purl and leave the stitch on the needle. Next, go through the first stitch on the back needle as if to knit—leave this stitch on the needle. Keeping the working yarn below the needles, work 2 sts on the front needle, followed by 2 sts on the back needle across the row as follows: On front needle, go through the first st as if to knit and drop it off the needle. Go through the second st as if to knit and leave it on the needle. Tighten the yarn. On the back needle, go through the first st as if to purl and drop it off the needle. Go through second st as if to knit and leave it on the needle. Tighten the yarn. When there is only one stitch on one needle, go through the front stitch as if to drop it off the needle. Go through the back stitch as if to purl and drop it off the needle. Pull the tail to the inside and weave in.

Resources

Debbie Bliss Yarns
www.knittingfever.com

Jamieson & Smith Ltd
www.jamiesonsshetland.co.uk

Lana Grossa
www.lanagrossa.com

Louisa Harding Yarns
www.knittingfever.com

Noro Yarns
www.knittingfever.com

Rowan Yarns
www.knitrowan.com

Twilleys
www.twilleys.co.uk